THE WONDERS & RICHES OF GOD'S WILL

Dakarabor O. David

Acknowledgment

I am using this medium to appreciate; God for
the grace given to me to serve as an inspiration to
the body of Christ and the world in general.
My inestimable angel David Folasade Ruth: for her
immense support and encouraging words.
Mr Agboola Yemi: who has demonstrated excellence
and diligence in the edition of this piece of material.
The body of Christ worldwide that thrive daily to
accomplish God's will on earth. May God bless you all.

Copyright

CONTACT:
discoverypointconsult@gmail.com | 08034694258

Preface

God expects us to have a burning desire to know His will, a consistent refire to pursue God's will and also, dare to die for His will. God is real as well as His will. You can know, pursue and fulfill it. We are not redeemed to practice guess work and grope in darkness as we look up to knowing God and serving Him in our daily endeavours. God's will is close to you. It is all encompassing; it covers every area of your life.

You cannot know true satisfaction in times of difficulty, connection amidst impossibilities and divine direction at every interval except you are passionate about God's programme and you surrender all to do His will.

Your life is a finished product of God's will. He has programmed every stage of your life to suit His will. That is why we do not live by imitation, assumption and mere emotion. We live in the revelation of God's will, which is the standard of a fulfilled life. It is not limited to marriage, business or the things that interest you most. They are things you do that gladden God's heart and it is built on His word and the leading of His Spirit.

Eternity will celebrate those who endeavoured to follow through on God's will. As you grow in grace and in the knowledge of God's word, you discover that perfection is central in God's will at every point of your life. You do not need to lobby neither do you need to struggle, all you need is to seek and pursue His will and be what he has purposed for you. This is what takes a man from the dust of nobody to the pinnacle of productivity and prosperity without cutting corners. And it takes us to the peak of sacrificial service.

In the light of the above, God wants us to understand in Ps 40:7-9 that "sacrifice and

offering thou" (He God) "didst not desire..." (To obey His will is better than sacrifice.) "Mine ears hast thou opened". (God daily opens our ears to know His will). "Then said I, Lo, I come: in the volume of the book it is written of me". Our knowledge of God's will is supposed to make us come before God in:

C - Consecration,

O - Obedience,

M - Motivated spirit, with

E - Endurance.

We must see ourselves positioned to do God's will. This demands that we firmly strive to fulfill every page of God's purpose for our lives. We must be like our Lord who fulfilled all the pages of God's programme for His life.

Chapter One

DEFINITION OF GOD'S WILL

God's will is that divine occurrence ordained by God to be accomplished by Himself or through certain individuals from different races or generations. A clear understanding of God's will assist you as an individual to know if you are heading the right way or whether you are going astray.

Walking step by step in the will of God in every area of your life makes you an achiever of God's purpose. It enables you to live a life that is full of wonderful and glorious experiences. You may be confused because I said doing the will of God enables you to enjoy glorious experiences when you think of saints that have been killed for their faith, properties that have been lost, children that have been slaughtered and resources that have been wasted just because God's people made up their mind to do God's will.

You do not need to be confused, as Christians we are pilgrims on earth, this world is not our home. Certainly, we will leave this world. But the mode of our departure is what we do not know. Whether through natural death, religious conflict or rapture is what we do not know. So, God can decide to take us to His kingdom through any of the means mentioned earlier. Our focus is that we are standing for God's will which makes us a channel of blessing and beneficiaries of that glorious city called Heaven. The Bible says, *"If any man serve me (does His will) let him follow me; and where I am, there shall also my servant be: if any man serve me, him will my Father honour"*

More so, your definition of that word with five letters, "g-l-o-r-y" matters. If you see glory as enjoying the privilege that the world may offer without any cross, then you do not have the understanding of glory from Christ's perspective. For Christ, going to the cross to die a death of shame, agony and rejection is the door into eternal glory.

God's will is revealed to make us partners in executing His purpose on earth. In order to help you maximize God's will for your life, I will expatiate on it with the word DEFINITION. It is:

D- Demanding

E- Eternal

F- Fathomless

I -Inspiring

N- Non negotiable

I-Incredible

T-Tactical

I-Immaculate

O-Organized

N- Noticeable

God's will is Demanding (It requires certain things): God's will, though interesting is demanding. The fact that God uses the knowledge of His will to train, test and transform us into the image of Christ makes it sometimes demanding. Jesus went to the cross, Paul was imprisoned, Moses faced Pharaoh and the Apostles were persecuted to fulfill God's will. At creation, God's programme to create the world demanded time, authority, unity and orderliness.

Time: It took God the Father, Son and Holy Spirit six days to create the world. God expects that you discern His timing while you pursue His will. Immediate action was demanded from Ananias when he was sent to Saul, Moses when he was sent to Egypt, Jonah when he was sent to Nineveh, e.t.c. while God's will to give Isaac to Abraham, brought the Israelites out of Egypt and take them to Canaan, make Joseph a governor and make David a king all took time. There is need to sacrifice time if you are passionate in doing God's will.

Authority: Everything on earth except man came into manifestation at God's command. In the same way, He commands His blessing upon our store houses (Deut 28:8a), the widow and the raven to feed Elijah (1 Kings 17:6, 9), Joshua to be strong and courageous (Josh 1:9a) Ezekiel to prophesy to the dry bones (Ezekiel 37:7). You must be ready to submit to God's authority while you aim at accomplishing His will. Avoid emotions and wrong counsels that will make you run ahead of God and miss His programme for your life.

Unity: Gen 3:29a"And *God said, Let us make man in our image...*" Unity is power. It creates a platform for cooperation and understanding. God revealed the indispensability of unity in accomplishing His will. Therefore, we are not to permit grudge between us and our spouses or family members as we aim at doing God's will. Certainly your spouse or family member may not be in agreement with you initially, your attitude, closeness and consistent communication will give them a little knowledge of how God leads and relates with you. Then they will start to support and encourage you when challenges come.

Orderliness: *"And God said, Let there be light: and there was light"* Gen 1:3. God's will demands orderliness. He appreciates those who are orderly in their pursuit of His will. Do not replace knowledge with zeal because when zeal is controlled by knowledge it produces a healthy passion that steadfastly hold on to character while striving for God's will. This eventually leads to perfection of God's purpose for our lives.
Courage, patience, faith and wisdom are other virtues needed to accomplish God's will.

GOD'S WILL IS ETERNAL: A close look into what God did from Genesis to Revelation reveals that He does not get involved in any project that has nothing to do with eternity. Why did He reject Ishmael from being the heir of promise? It was because the process of his birth and the lineage of his mother contradicted the pattern God intended to use to raise an heir for Abraham. God's will was that Abraham's heir should come from

Sarah. God neglected Abraham for 13 years because of Ishmael's birth. God only decided to expand Ishmael as a result of Abraham's prayer in Gen. 17:18. However, He maintained His ground that His eternal purpose concerning Abraham's heir would not be altered by Abraham's mistake.

Does your pursuit have anything to do with God's eternal purpose? Those whose ambition correlates with God's eternal purpose will receive eternal reward.

GOD'S WILL IS FATHOMLESS: Some people have rejected Jesus based on their belief that God is not married and as such cannot have a child. They being ignorant are trying to find out God. Using your limited understanding of natural and earthly experiences to find out God will make you a fool. It is hard to find out God when He is set to achieve His purpose in the life of an individual or in a nation. If you are among those who never move until they have a full knowledge of God's will you may not go far in experiencing God's fullness in life and ministry.

When God told Abraham to come out of his father's house in Gen 12:1 and sacrifice Isaac in Gen 22:1, he obeyed despite the fact that he was not privy to God's plan and God poured out His blessings on him.

For instance, God can direct you to marry someone who is not as rich and as handsome as you want or does not seem to have all the qualities you cherish. It may be difficult initially to accept his proposal, but as you humble yourself and accept such an individual, God's purpose becomes clearer and you find peace, progress and prosperity which makes the union pleasurable, productive and perfect will for your life.

I learnt of a lame man that was led to marry a rich Christian lady. When the man told her pastor, he could not relay the message to the lady because he envisaged that the lady will not accept such a proposal. However, because of the man's persistence, the pastor told the lady. As if the pastor knew her mind, she withdrew from the church being dissatisfied that God had not given her the man of her dreams. Thank God for that pastor, he prayerfully pursued and persuaded her to obey God. Though it took him three years to get her convinced, she eventually gave in and obeyed God's demand. Surprisingly, on the day of their wedding, while they held themselves, the man being on a wheelchair, the bride groaned bitterly and silently prayed: "God, you led me into this marriage!" Then she pulled him up out of a heart full of pain. To the surprise of all, the man started walking, nobody knew even the pastor that God wanted to use the lady to put an end to the man's lameness.

You may think you have a rounded knowledge of God's will. But in most cases, a new page of wonder unfolds when you take the initial step to do His will. Joseph did not know he would get to the prison before becoming great in Egypt. No one knew that God's prophecy on the crucifixion of Christ in Gen 3:15 will take forty two (42) generations before it fulfillment.

GOD'S WILL IS INSPIRING: When God reveals His will, he inspires you so as to empower and position you to fulfill it.

People will challenge the motive behind your intention

which can affect your zeal if care is not taken. Amazingly, God keeps your passion alive by fueling your knowledge of His will through different means that inspires you. I remember my experience after I wrote my first book. I decided to neglect my passion for writing inspirational books because I did not get the needed encouragement. Fortunately as I went to the Lord in prayer, I received a revelation that served as a guide on what steps to take. As I obeyed, I met a lot of people who told me that the book was indeed a blessing. This made me happy and motivated.

GOD'S WILL IS NON-NEGOTIABLE: You can toy with man's will and go free but no one toys with God's will and gets away with it. It is extremely indispensable to man's life. A little diversion in most cases leads to regret. As Christians, the fulfillment of our destiny has a lot to do with daily observance of God's will.
If Joshua had enquired from the Israelites the method of war that will bring down the walls of Jericho, he would have gotten wonderful suggestions. But the method that gave them victory was simple and unusual.

Think about heaven, what is God's will (requirements) for those who wants to be partakers of its bliss and treasures. In John 14:6 Jesus says: *"...I am the way, the truth, and the life: no man cometh unto the Father, but by me"* and Heb 12:14 says: *"Follow peace with all men, and holiness, without which no man shall see the Lord:"* If you decide to engage yourself in any other activity like giving alms, praying, being gentle, e.t.c without due consideration of the fact that you must give your life to Jesus and be holy before entering heaven, such an individual will be disappointed.

GOD'S WILL IS INCREDIBLE: God specializes in surprises. Innumerable event in history has proved that God's thoughts and ways are different from that of man. It is common to man be it in the church or in the world to appoint people into positions of authority based on their educational and financial strength. God did not consider financial, societal and material status before He chose David to replace Saul neither was Mary a great woman in the society before God honoured her to be the mother of the Messiah. What about Paul? Who would have thought he would write half of the New Testament, establish more churches than Peter and set the stage of an unlimited ministry in the Gentile world? But God chose and used him. Think of Joseph, the earthly father of Jesus, who knew he would be the one in David's lineage to activate the promise of the Messiah, only God. And there is nothing as astonishing as when God told the children of Israel to go forward with the red sea before them and Pharaoh behind them. Yet, that was the way to their triumphant entry into the promised land.

A lot of things happen in life that are beyond one's reasoning. These prove that God will forever be God. Therefore, all we need to do is to follow His direction even when we seem not to fully understand.

GOD'S WILL IS TACTICAL: In Deut 18:18a God said *"I will raise them up a Prophet from among their brethren, like unto thee* (Moses) ..."This prophecy kept Israel in earnest expectation of the Messiah. But God tactically arranged it that John the Baptist should be the forerunner of Jesus.

No one thought that someone will come before Jesus until it was prophesied in Malachi 4:5-6.

I learnt from the book of Exodus that God is tactical in achieving His goals and nothing moves Him to change His plan except in few occasions. To start with, it was His will that the Israelites should go down to Egypt and He aimed at making use of Joseph to accomplish that. Initially, it seemed as if it will not come to pass but in the end God worked it out and Joseph got to the highest level of leadership in Egypt. The fact that he was used to rescue Egypt and many other nations from famine made it possible for him to bring his family members to Egypt. And as such fulfilled the promise God gave Abraham in Gen 15: 13. Based on God's programme in Gen 15:14a, another king came who was not happy with the presence and favour of God on the Israelites, so, he made them servants. Fulfilling the second part of God's plan in verse 14a. When it was time to fulfill verse 14b God gave them Moses. However, when Moses went to Pharaoh, he increased their suffering. As a result of that the children of Israel wished they should remain in Egypt forever. I expected God to hastily propel Pharaoh to release them but He ensured that all He told Moses in Exodus 7:3-5 were fulfilled before the Israelites were released. A little wonder God kept quiet while the Israelites were shouting as a result of increased affliction, until He judged Pharaoh and His armies in the sea.

The question that we should ask ourselves is if Moses was not there the Israelites would have hindered God from bringing them out of Egypt. As Christians, whenever we are persecuted because of our faith in God, let us be rest assured that God will tactically intervene. Amidst those seemingly delay, He will work out His plan for your life in Jesus name. Amen.

GOD'S WILL IS IMMACULATE: God had willed from Genesis to send a Saviour to save the generality of humanity. The yardstick of the ministry of the Messiah was revealed for easy identification. Many people came before the arrival of Jesus but their lives could not match the standard that was specified, but immediately Jesus appeared, everyone knew that he was indeed, the saviour of the world. Though, he had a lot of issues with the religious leaders of his days, yet, everything that was written concerning the Messiah was fulfilled in him. One of such verses is Isaiah 61:1 *"THE SPIRIT of the Lord God is upon me; because the Lord hath anointed me to preach good tidings unto the meek; he hath sent me to bind up the broken hearted, to proclaim liberty to the captives, and the opening of the prison to them that are bruised."* And it was fulfilled in Luke 4: 16. Though, some sect will claim that Jesus is not the Saviour of the world, even Pontius Pilate confirmed it. So, whenever God wants to do something, he makes it clear.

Think of marriage for instance, many youths find it difficult to pray through and find the will of God for their lives. Many of them are depending on permutation. If I give the brother or sister a signal through my eyes or body and constantly visit him or her, I believe he or she will give in and marry me. Though most of the present day God's will in marriage were gotten in this manner, nevertheless, whenever God wants a man to marry a woman, He reveals it in a clear way. Some people may want to argue, but beneficiaries of such marriages can attest to it. Parties to such marriages find it difficult to resist and those who do, live to regret. An important quality you find in God ordained marriages is love. It solidifies the foundation of such marriages making it capable to stand any storm, but permutation marriages fall apart when difficulties arise.

GOD'S WILL IS ORGANIZED: When I took a close look into everything Jesus did. I discovered that God organizes occurrences in our lives to suit His purpose. When Jesus was to feed five thousand, a boy was there to give five loaves and two fishes, when he was to fulfill the scripture concerning his triumphant entry into Jerusalem, the ass he needed was already waiting for him. The great lesson we need to learn is that even though Jesus knew where the ass was, he did not request for it before the appointed time.

Why is it that many believers go into pre-marital sex? It is because they do not want to be organized. You should not be so impatient or spiritually weak to the point of going into pre-marital sex. Those who are into courtship or are having just a day to their marriage should be more careful because that is not a yard stick for pre-marital sex.

You will also discover that when Jesus needed a place for the Lord supper it was made available and at his death Joseph of Aramathaea gave him a befitting burial as prophesied in Isaiah 53:9 *"He made his grave…with the rich in his death"*. He never got to a point when what he needed to fulfill his purpose was not available. I decree that as you set out to fulfill God's will for your life everything needed will be available in Jesus name. Amen.

Many people reject God's will as a result of fear of failure. They assume that their destiny cannot be fulfilled if they wholeheartedly follow God. They ignore God's call for a specific divine assignment such as being a pastor, evangelist and so on. Remember, he promised hundredfold accomplishments for those who give their all for His will.

A brother testified about what God did during his wedding. The little money he had was used for the traditional wedding. Therefore, he was left with nothing for the church wedding. He said when it was two days before the wedding, he felt like collapsing, but God proved his faithfulness and sent help in the evening of that day from various places. And the remnant of what they had sustained them for a month before he got a job. I shared this testimony to encourage those who are of marriageable age and are delaying because of money. Be rest assured that God who revealed her to you has programmed provision that will sustain the marriage, because *"Whoso findeth a wife findeth a good thing, and obtaineth favour of the LORD"* Prov 18:22.

GOD'S WILL IS NOTICEABLE Something unique about God's will in every area of man's endeavour is that it is noticeable. When Jesus was in his mother's womb, Elizabeth noticed him; at His birth, the wise men were notified; at twelve, the Pharisees and Sadducees testified of his knowledge and at His baptism, John the Baptist acknowledged Him; when he said, *"Behold the Lamb of God, which taketh away the sin of the world"* John 1:29b. God used innumerable experiences of Christ to notify humanity that he was indeed the Messiah. Even the unrepentant soldiers at his grave were notified of his majestic status when the angel rolled the stone at His sepulcher and sat upon it.

In the same way, great ministers have had the opportunity of an expanded ministry through divinely inspired publicity of their services and crusades which make sinners and saints alike to join their congregation. More so, God has a way of notifying His children ahead concerning certain decisions He would want them to take to facilitate the perfection of His purpose for their lives. Be it in the area of business, family or ministry. He does this through words of knowledge, visions and dreams. A good example was when God told Joseph in a dream not to put Mary away, when she was conceived of the Holy Ghost.

However, we learn by making mistakes but when God shines the light of His mercy upon us he intervenes immediately as He discovers we are about to make a mistake that would waste our money or change His perfect purpose for our lives. That was what He did for Balaam but he rejected God's intervention because of covetousness. If you have a burning desire to do God's will coupled with persistent prayer to know His will, He will definitely reveal His will to you in all things.

The problem of many people is that they are not observant enough to discern God's plan. Such was Elimelech who hastily left Judah with his wife Naomi and their children because of famine. He lost his life and that of his children. We should be mature enough in any given situation to take note of God's will. Our decisions should not be centered on conveniences but on committing ourselves to attain God's agenda.

Finally, I have discovered since I got saved that God reveals his love to you by making His will known. Be smart to maximize it.

Chapter Two

INSIGHT INTO GOD'S WILL

The difference in each aspect of man's life requires insight that will position man to fully accomplish God's will within the limited time available.

Some of these aspects are;

1. Salvation
2. Sanctification
3. Spirit baptism
4. Educational pursuit
5. Choice of institution
6. Place of settlement
7. Marriage
8. Ministry

GOD'S WILL FOR OUR SALVATION

1 Peter 3:9 states that *"The Lord is not slack concerning his promise, but is long suffering to us ward, not willing that any should perish, but that all should come to repentance."* God's greatest desire is the salvation of man. He paid the most precious price of Christ's blood to make provision for our salvation. He only blesses the work of our hands to

enrich us, but sacrificed His only begotten Son to redeem us. Therefore, He expects proper response of repentance from us in appreciation of His love. The level of man's degeneration as a result of Adams fall makes salvation inevitable. If you are happy being a beneficiary of God's creation why should you not maximize His provision for the salvation of your soul that ushers you into an endless and blissful eternity which required the blood of His Son. Think of evangelists who have died for the gospel's sake, saints who are praying for your salvation and millions that is spent to bring the gospel to you and take a corresponding action.

GOD'S WILL FOR YOUR SANCTIFICATION

"Blessed are the pure in heart: for they shall see God" Sanctification is God's heart beat. It is easy to receive healing or breakthrough without purity but you will not be received into paradise without sanctification. This is the second work of grace that Jesus prayed in John 17:17. The Israelites were told to sanctify themselves so they could experience wonders in the days of Joshua, which means they must avoid all unrighteousness. Therefore, we must avoid sin so that God can sanctify us. Your anticipation for sanctification experience should be more than that of your earnest expectation or cravings for marriage.

SANCTIFICATION AND YOUR FULFILLMENT

You cannot accomplish God's fullness for your life without sanctification. It gives access into deeper riches of God's fullness and solidifies your Christian profession. It is not easy for Satan to sidetrack a sanctified vessel from God's will for his or her live.

Those who feel entire sanctification is not necessary to access the fullness of God's will for their lives should remember that Saul sinned and his kingdom was taken from him; Moses smote the rock twice in annoyance and he missed the promise land, and Samson lost his ministry as a result of immorality. A lot of things will emanate to entangle you and eliminate your passion for God. It takes sanctification to remain established in the pursuit of God's purpose for your life.

Think about a minister who kept malice with his denomination because they brought someone who was younger than him in the faith to lead in place of the former provincial or regional leader. Though the minister was told to lead a particular section of the church, He was so annoyed that he secretly planned to leave the church and establish his own ministry with a heart full of malice. He decided to move to another place upon completion of his house. So, a sendforth party was conducted for him without any body's knowledge that he was going to set up his own church. It was surprising to the church when information came that he has left the church. As a young convert, I went to my friend's house and met them discussing the issue without any concern as if what he did was alright. It did not take long when he died a terrible death. Who knew whether he will still be alive if he had not left the church in annoyance? This reaffirms the position of purity of heart. God wants you to prioritize it. It is a sustaining force to anything we get from God.

Are there not people who said that their marriage was God's will and yet ended in divorce? You may say demons caused it. I can bear witness that demons cannot manipulate two sanctified believers at the same time to the point that they cannot forgive and forget when offended. We must seek sanctification before any other thing. It increases God's presence in our lives, enable us overcome temptation and gives us victory over any test that comes our way.

GOD'S WILL AND SPIRIT BAPTISM

Man was naturally endowed with power at creation to dominate the world. But such opportunity was withdrawn due to Adam's fall. Nevertheless, Jesus credited man's account with power from the moment he manifested Himself on earth. An account in the scripture that confirms the position of the new man is Luke 10:19 when Jesus said *"... I give unto you power over all the power...of the enemy and nothing shall by any means hurt you."* This power brought restoration of authority to man. So, the new man is not expected to react to situation or challenges in fear or anxiety like the old man. Furthermore, the book of Acts gives a vivid record of the new man operating in the newness of God's power.

In a nutshell, the new man (the believer);

1. Receives God's fullness. Acts 2:1-4,
2. Restores thousands of souls to Christ. Acts 2:41,
3. Raises the lame. Acts 3:6-8,
4. Reaffirms his purpose. Acts 4:19-20,
5. Releases God's judgement on sinners. Acts 5:3-5, 9.
6. Represents God before men. Acts 6:9-10,
7. Rekindles joy on earth. Acts 8:5-8,
8. Reveals the superiority of Christ. Acts 9:8-12,
9. Rends heaven Act 16:25-26,

10. Reproduces Christ ministry. Acts 19: 10-12.

11. Revives the dead. Acts 9:40.

God is earnestly willing to empower you so you can achieve more for him. He said *"he that believeth on me the works that I do shall he do also and greater works than these shall he do because I go to my Father"* But this power cannot manifest in your life without;

P- Persistent prayer.

O- Obedience to God.

W- Wholehearted consecration.

E- Enduring thirst.

R- Resolute faith.

GOD'S WILL AND YOUR ACADEMIC PURSUIT

When I first gave my life to Christ, God gave me a revelation concerning my ministry which made me confused. So, I sought counsel from my leader to know if I could go to the missionary school straight away. But he advised that I should further my education. I did not have the opportunity to go to the university directly therefore, I went to a college of education. Even though, God told me to go to the college of education nearby, I did not feel like. After staying at home for another year, I reluctantly picked up the admission. To my surprise, when I got there, I saw the hand of God in action. I became the General Coordinator of my fellowship for three years, learnt how to address a large number of people, received the key to write books and became exposed to a lot of training and challenges on leadership.

Most youth lose focus easily, they claim that they do not

need to further their education because God wants to use them. Moses was learned in all the knowledge of Egypt and Daniel had the knowledge to function as an authority in Babylon. Without education how should he have understood the writing of Jeremiah that propelled him to pray for the freedom of Israel? Modern day youths should be aware that God is highly interested in their academic pursuit and desires that they attain excellence. More so, it is possible for God to lead you to a particular institution if you seek His face when seeking for admission into the university. Though, God still work out His will in the lives of those who were not exposed to the fact that they need to seek the face of God before making a choice about the university they are to attend and the course to study. This is because "...*all things work together for good to them that love God and are called according to His purpose.*" (Romans 8:38)

Earlier on I talked about salvation, sanctification and the Holy Ghost baptism which demands that you lay all on the altar. Most people shy away as a result of this. They assume that the commitment that follows consecration will result into failure. By God's grace, Pastor Olukoya, Pastor Myles Munroe, Pastor Kenneth E Agins, Pastor W.F Kumuyi, Pastor E.A Adeboye and many others have committed themselves to God and have become the epitome of excellence in this generation. If you have given your life to Christ and He calls you into a greater ministry do not reject such neither should you abandon your educational pursuit.

Education is information. If you are not informed, you will be deformed. It prepares you to prime, prune and provide indelible impact on pilgrims of this age who are pressed with diverse realities in the modern world. A sound knowledge in English language for instance, will give you access into most countries in the world. The audience of this generation evaluates your presentation from its introduction to its conclusion. With sound educational background, you will have extra edge in your presentation. It facilitates the interest of your audience and brings warmth acceptance of the message if it was soaked with prayers. I do not mean it should be more of vocabularies that require dictionary before it can be comprehended. People do not come with dictionary to public gatherings except the ones on their phones. So, you will be considered a clown due to grammatical aggrandisement. You can be systematic and logical, and yet, simple in your ministrations.

GOD'S WILL AND YOUR PLACE OF WORK OR SETTLEMENT

There is a land flowing with milk and honey that God has provided for everyone. Therefore, your place of settlement should connect you with the milk and honey that God has programmed for you.

Abraham was greatly loved by God and had that generational status of being the friend of God. Yet, God did not solidify His friendship with him until he left his father's land. Similarly, God has prepared a place for you if you care to ask Him. Majority may be of the opinion that you should not bother God with your place of settlement, because "*all things work together for good for those who love God*" But God told Isaac not to go to Egypt when there was a famine in Canaan. He had a hundred percent fold due to obedience.

As Christians, you must be mindful of God's leading as you attempt settling in a place for ministry, marriage or career pursuit. My leader in Deeper Life Campus Fellowship testified how he came to the campus. He said after he had prayed to God for a job, he dreamt and saw a lady calling him to come to their campus to help them. He did not know how to connect that dream, until he saw an advertisement of a lecturing job on a paper that was used to wrap something for someone. When he applied, he got the job. The Sister he saw in his dream was the one who helped him to get accommodation and they started DLCF (Deeper Life Campus Fellowship) on that campus together.

Pastor Adeboye also testified about his experience when he was to do his doctorate degree. He said he went for a scholarship interview so he could study abroad and was able to answer all the questions. But unfortunately, the head of those who conducted the interview was asleep during the interview. When he woke up, he asked a question outside Mathematics and Pastor Adeboye told him that the question was outside the scope of where questions should be generated. So, he was not given the scholarship. As God would have it, on his way out of the venue for the scholarship, he met someone who knew his worth in Mathematics and he advised him to go to University of Lagos. Fortunately, that was where he worked as a lecturer and later received God's call and now has the largest church in Africa. In the scripture;
Abraham was led to Canaan;
David was told to remain in Judah;

Joseph was led to Egypt;
Joseph was told to take Jesus to Egypt to protect him from Herod.

THE SIGNIFICANCE OF WHERE YOU LIVE/ WORK AND YOUR FULFILLMENT

A close look into your place or organization of settlement and God's will reveal that;

1. It is a place of Learning.

God in his mercy systematically leads us to places where we can learn virtues, strategies, languages, principles or things that prepare us to accomplish God's purpose for our lives. Learning increases your knowledge and experience; experience wisdom; wisdom usefulness and usefulness relevance. Joseph learnt management in Potiphar's house and was empowered to manage Egypt's wealth. Daniel learnt how to receive answers to difficult questions through divine wisdom and he was able to interpret Nebuchadnezzar's dreams. He became skilled in interpretation of dreams which enabled him to give an account of world events from Nebuchadnezzar's era to Christ millennial reign. Someone like Pastor Sunday Adelaja would not have easily achieved his purpose if he has not learnt their language in Kjiv.

2. It is a place of Service.

Your level of effectiveness will greatly depend on the knowledge you have gathered while serving. That is why organizations request for your years of experience in your field or career. It is believed that it can amount to wealth of experience which could be in your ministerial endeavour, spiritual growth or career development. Where you reside/work has some level of influence on your life, likewise in your service for the Lord. Diligence in service produces distinction in understanding, creativity in reasoning and clarity in planning.

The organization or denomination you settle with will present opportunity to serve. Your worth, wealth of knowledge, attitude to work and the level of impart are measured in quantifiable terms. God uses the period of serving to train us. Jacob learnt the best way to raise healthy cattle while serving; Joseph learnt management in Potiphar's house, Paul mastery of the Law of Moses to mention a few. Some organizations for instance, may not pay as much as you expect but God divinely allows or instructs His children to remain in such organizations for a given period of time to learn and use their potential profitably. You can never attain exponential development without serving. So, while you are thinking of the organization to settle with, I want you to understand that such organization or denomination will afford you the opportunity to maximize your potential like Joseph which will definitely position you to fulfill God's programme for your life to the latter. But anywhere you are influenced negatively or enforced to cheat, commit immorality, join a cult in the name of promotion and totally abandon your ministry as a child of God cannot be a place that God has programmed for you to settle. Be it a church, an organization or where you want to reside.

3. It is a place of Test.
Everyone who thirsts after God's fullness will be tested. Man's emotion detests being tested. Yet, account in history has proved that you become approved of God, solidified in your pursuit of God's will and inspired to go higher in your field of career when you pass your test.

Therefore, you must expect test on your way up. Your patience, conviction, potential, knowledge, and virtues will be tested. Those who are not ready for test may not get to their destination in life.

These tests vary:

- Joseph was tested with fornication and imprisonment.
- Abraham was tested to sacrifice Isaac,
- David was tempted to kill Saul.
- The Rechabites were tested with alcohol.
- Meshach, Shadrach and Abednego were tested with fire.
- Daniel was tested with lions.

The test may be projected to move you from the point of God's glory and visitation for your life. This is why we should not take decisions based on our feelings but on divine guidance and faith.

I learnt of a woman who was denied of her promotion for twelve years. Fortunately, she was the brains behind the ideas that gave others promotion in her department. She became very sad because her hard work was not rewarded. Those she told her idea ran with it and were enjoying the dividend of her insight. She felt like quitting the job but later thought of taking it to God in prayer. God cannot fail, when her promotion came it took her six levels higher. This is contrary to their mode of promotion in which you are taken a level higher and you are expected to serve for some time before another one comes. She was fortunate to climb six levels at a goal. This is the picture of the test that drives a lot of people from where God wants them to be at a particular moment.

4. It is a place of Influence.

If God wants you to settle for anything except sin, He makes you influential in it. Don Moen influences millions through his songs; Mount Zion Films in Nigeria influences a lot of Christians through their films and John Maxwell influences a lot of people with his exceptional knowledge and insight on leadership. You may not start from the point of influence but with time, you will become influential be it in a church, an organization or a chosen career. This does not mean you will be the head of such an organization if that is not God's plan for your life.

5. It is a place of Connection.

God specializes in connecting his children who seek His counsel before settling in a church, organization or environment. Elisha was given a house by the Shunamite woman because he passed her house often. The lame man at the beautiful gate received healing because he was always at the beautiful gate whenever Peter and John went in for prayer. We must pray that God should divinely lead us to an organization, environment or chosen career that will connect us to the center of God's plan for our lives.

Remember, Joseph could not have had access to Pharaoh's palace without serving Potiphar. His decision to send Joseph to prison promoted him to the platform of his connection with the buckler that connected him to Pharaoh. In most cases, where or what you settle for has a way of making a difference in your life. The connection may not come when you expect but as you continue serving the Lord and exercising faith on his promises, you discover that God's leading concerning where and what you settle for will take a step higher if not ten steps higher spiritually, ministerially, maritally and career wise.

6. It is a place of Usefulness.

The focus point of this book is to help you maximize the will of God for your life. Some people decide to settle for things or environment that minimizes God's purpose for their lives. Because God sometimes withhold certain information from those who do not bother to seek counsel from Him, they assume that anything they do is the best they could have done. Not until you learn to carry God along in all things, you will never know your position as regards God's will for your life.

I want you to know that God has designed you for a purpose to fulfill His will in a given place at a given time if you are His child. I always tell graduates that their job opportunity awaits them where God has programmed to use them. Every graduate must pray that God will take them to their place of usefulness. Most of the connection you need in life awaits you there. Joseph was useful in Potiphar's house, in the prison and in Pharaoh's palace.

More so, God uses you at different levels and in different places because your life in God is in stages. Each stage of your life carries different purposes in God and assignment to different people. That someone is in America today does not mean that God cannot send him to Africa or anywhere in the world tomorrow.

7. It is a place where you hear from God.

Those who consistently obey God's directive hear from Him always. On the other hand, those who grieve His spirit will be abandoned to themselves which will lead to spiritual stagnancy.

Jonah found himself in the fish belly because he refused to go to where God sent him. Those who saw him going to Nineveh never knew he was not supposed to be in the ship until the flood came. He never heard from God again till he repented and agreed to obey God. Another person who did not hear from God based on the action he took was Abraham. God left him for thirteen years because he obeyed his wife and impregnated Hagar. If you are in the right place doing the right thing, God will always minister to you such that you will remain fresh in your spirit and updated concerning God's call for your life.

God will always speak to you if He is the brain behind your decision because He knows that your life is anchored in Him. Involvement in evangelistic outreach, engaging in spiritual warfare, giving to the needy and seeking His face for divine guidance are ways of boosting your possibility of hearing from God.

GOD'S WILL AND YOUR MARRIAGE

The sensitivity of marriage makes it central in God's heart. It produces hope, happiness, health, help and all round harvest. The change that humanity has experienced is a product of fruitfulness in marriage. Every phase of God's creation calls our attention to the indispensability of marriage. It may surprise you that without marriage there would be no

M- Moses (He brought out Israel from Slavery)
A- Abraham (The origin of our relationship with God)

R- Rebekah (Who gave birth to Israel
R - Rahab who hid the spies Joshua sent to Jericho
I-Isaac (The promised child)
A- Amos. (One of the Prophets)
G- Great Inventors (Whose invention pave way for modernization)
E- Elijah (who restored Israel to God from the worship of Baal)

Marriage is not supposed to be handled carelessly. It requires proper consideration and supplication. This is because the hope of our fathers, the answers to the prayers of this and many generations and the prophetic writings of the scriptures cannot be fulfilled without marriage. In God's programme, He has positioned your marriage to fill a gap and accomplish a purpose that is presently unknown to many around you. Such was the marriage of Joseph and Mary, the earthly parents of Jesus.

Those in the world may limit marriage to a place where food, laundry and pleasure are provided. This is just 30% of God's purpose for marriage. Majority who made those things the peak of their expectation in marriage end up in regret. Some even go as far as divorcing. A lot of things have fallen apart because people despise the will of God in marriage. Your purpose and eternity should be the determinant of your marriage. As a result of the uncertainties associated with marriage, the Bible warns *"Be ye not unequally yoked together with unbelievers; for what fellowship hath righteousness with unrighteousness? And what communion hath light with darkness?"* 2 Corinthians 6:14. This warning must be given attention. God wants His children to get married to people of like faith. Many have fallen into the hands of false brethren because they paid less attention to this warning. An individual without the fear of God can change at any time. So, anyone who marries such is gambling with their future. The Bible also confirmed that *"riches are inheritance from fathers while a good wife or husband is from the Lord."* He is not willing that you regret your marriage which makes Him to make Himself available to guide and direct your footsteps towards marrying the right person.

Ingredients Found In God Ordained Marriages

1. Love,
2. Understanding,
3. Unity,
4. Submission,
5. Contentment,

Love: Love is an indispensable element that determines whether a marriage will last or not. First Corinthians thirteen gives us a clear picture of a life of love. Our Lord Jesus also revealed the major attribute of true love when he said *"No love is more than this that a man should lay down his life for his friends"* John 15: 15. True love lays down something for the other party. Many replace love with emotional feelings. Though, it is part of it but it is not all of it. When God leads you to marry an individual that you never thought of marrying, it takes love for God to obey. What I have discovered is that people you find it difficult to marry initially, may be, because they are not from your tribe or they were once strict in dealing with you, probably as your leader in the church, such later appear to be the right person when you agree to marry them. Just be sure God is the one leading you.

True love understands, it is peaceful, kind, accommodating, strong and caring. You must also understand that a love that is from God avoids things that annoy God. If you tolerate sex before marriage, you annoy God and any man or woman who makes sex before marriage the condition for marrying you is not the will of God for you in marriage. You must watch out for love because it helps you and your partner to plan, pray, play, dine, tackle problems and resolve dispute together.

How can you identify pretenders who will change when they get home?
Prayer is the key. Never accept a proposal without spending quality time in prayers. Many men have married agents of darkness because they did not pray enough before going into such marriages. God will reveal the true identity of the man or woman if you seek His face before taking decision. Your purpose and eternity is more important than the pleasure that blind many people's eyes from the realities in marriage.

Understanding: Understanding is the bedrock for peaceful coexistence in marriage. The first thing Satan attacks in marriages is the understanding of the couple. He is aware of its relevance. Understanding guarantees the fortification of the spiritual strength of marriages and solidification of the unity between couples. The possibility experienced by Nimrod at the tower of Babel can only be enjoyed in a family where understanding reigns. When God puts communication barrier between those that were building the tower of Babel the project seized. So also, misunderstanding destroys the progress of most couples until understanding is enthroned.

I learnt of a couple who were fighting each other. The man was planning to marry another wife and this made the woman to rain curses him. When things were becoming difficult for him he went for prayer and some people told him that his mother was possessed. He asked his mother and she confirmed it. He never knew that his problem was not from his mother. Fortunately, he went to a man of God who told him to send for his wife. When she got there the man of God asked the woman the man's offense and she responded that the husband had never bought a gift for her since they married and that he was going about planning to marry another woman, therefore, he would never prosper. The man of God settled their dispute and told him to buy gifts for her. Immediately he bought her a bag, his way opened. Someone he once worked with called him and said he just felt he was supposed to give him something for his labour and he gave him five million naira (#5, 000 000) . The devil kept him struggling until the wall of misunderstanding in their family was broken.

Many battles are won through understanding in marriages. Let us not toy with it because it is a great weapon.

Unity: It amazes me when I see people go into marriage without considering the place of unity in such marriages. These are people who believe they can marry any lady and when she misbehaves, they will deal with her. If you cannot lay the foundation of being united with your wife, how can you be happy? Raise godly children? And make it to heaven?

One of the major causes of disunity is lack of financial resources. But lack of finance should not take peace away from your family. The same power that made the two of you to be one will work out divine provision if two of you will unite in love, prayer and obedience to God.

Another cause of disunity is self. Some couples find it difficult to sacrifice for each other. Anywhere selfishness reigns, disunity will be the order of the day. We must not desire anything at the detriment of the other person. We must jointly take decision and bear any form of inconvenience together whenever sacrifice is needed.

More so, do not allow major decisions in your family to be pioneered by your parents. It weakens the cord of unity in the family. God may sometimes use them to give advice that will provide solution to a difficult situation. Notwithstanding, such an approach should not be an everyday affair. The earlier each couple learns to take major decisions themselves, the better. It will position them to help their children in the future.

Submission: A willing submission is better than submission that is derived through domination. A willing submission is a product of love, care and oneness. While the latter is a product of force and threat. Any man who desires submission from the wife should ensure fervent love and honour towards the wife. This makes her cleave to you which make the relationship stronger. A woman whose heart is knitted to her husband submits to him. This is because she feels safe, secured and assured of fulfillment in life.

Contentment:If you give most people a piece of paper to write their wishes. You will be surprised what some people will pen down. A lot of people come into marriage with their wish list. Wish list is not bad but should not be given greater attention than the responsibility demanded from each partner to make the marriage a success. Any objective in our list should be handled with contentment, prayer, faith and patience.

Contentment keeps your hope alive because it removes worry and anxiety that produces impatience. It keeps you in the best state to plan your future and follow through on the success of your marriage. It also rescues it from undue friction from friends and in- laws.

When contentment is in place, each partner remains faithful to the marriage vow. Nothing steals their heart from the marriage. They live in the consciousness that God is extremely interested in their marriage and as such, they hold on to God's promises until they access everything that God has planned for their union.

Chapter Three

THE WONDERS OF GOD'S WILL

Wonders are events that amaze the generality of humanity. It sets the pace of a new dawn and a new realm of possibility. It adds uniqueness to life and attributes greatness to God. God specializes in doing wonders amongst men.

A systematic analysis of God's operation amongst men has revealed series of surprises relating to God's will for man.

Below are examples of such wonders;

- God left others and made Abraham the pathfinder of man's relationship with Him.
- Sarah gave birth to Isaac at 89
- The Israelites crossed the red sea
- Elijah went to heaven through a chariot of fire
- Meshach, Shadrach and Abednego walked in the fire
- Daniel slept with lions
- Mary conceived Jesus as a virgin
- At Christ crucifixion, the sun refused to shine

- The veil of the temple rend
- The earth quaked and the rocks rend

In a nutshell

- God's will is unstoppable.
- God's will is undeniable.
- God's will is irresistible.
- God's will is incontestable.
- God's will is unquestionable.
- God's will is unchangeable.

GOD'S WILL IS UNSTOPPABLE

One of the houses Christian bodies bought for Bible production is the house of a man who said the Bible will go into extinction in fifty (50) years' time while he was on earth. But God proved that His will is unstoppable. Instead, his house was used to produce millions of Bibles. The commissioning of Pastor E.A Adeboye follows the same supernatural feat of God's unstoppable power. He was chosen to succeed the founder of The Redeemed Christian Church of God when the founder was to pass on. There was uproar against that decision. The founder however sought the face of God concerning who should oversee the church after his departure; he did not allow the uproar to change his decision. He said when it is time, (as it is today that The Redeemed Christian Church of God is the largest and fastest growing church in Africa) they will see the reason why he chose him. Though Pastor E. A. Adeboye and his wife fasted and prayed that God will choose someone else since many people were striving for the position, the will of God still prevailed and He was ordained as the General Overseer of the church.

More so, Pastor W.F Kumuyi testified of how Deeper Christian Life Ministry was established in one of the towns in Edo State, Nigeria. They were resistant to the gospel, therefore, insisted that Deeper Christian Life Ministry should not be established in the area. Fortunately, the church organized a crusade in which people in the village partook. Amongst these people was a lame woman. God greatly moved in the crusade and many experienced the supernatural touch of God. On their way home, the woman began to cry because she did not receive her miracle. When they got to the village, everyone came down from the lorry except the lame woman. As God would have it. When people wanted to bring her down from the lorry, she rose up and began to walk. A two-day public holiday was declared and the church was invited to establish a location in that village. God's will is unstoppable!

REASONS WHY GOD'S WILL IS UNSTOPPABLE
God's will is unstoppable because of the following reasons;
1. It radiates God's glory.
2. It reveals God's grace.
3. It reaffirms God's greatness.

4. It represents God's genuineness.

It Radiates God's Glory:
God's will is His affirmation on any situation or decision. He never compromises His will because it radiates His

glory. God's glory reveals the finality of the position of His majestic authority. He takes great delight in His will for our lives and will never allow it to be covered. Whatsoever stops God's will in the life of God's children has in a way stopped the radiation of God's glory concerning that situation or individual. But for God's will to be accomplished we must consistently maintain holiness. The will of God has been stopped and His glory covered in the lives of many Christians who allowed sin while fighting spiritual battles. God was able to preserve His will for Jesus because Joseph heard from God and stopped his plan of putting Mary away and later took him to Egypt when Herod wanted to kill him.

A woman confessed how they killed a child who was to be like Pastor W.F. Kumuyi. They said they had been trailing the child from the womb because they saw his glory in the kingdom of darkness. They found it difficult to get the child because the parents were holy. Unfortunately, they manipulated them and caused a misunderstanding between them. They slept without settling the dispute. That opened the door for the enemies, so they came that night and killed the child who would have accomplished a powerful ministry. Yes, God's will is unstoppable but we must pray and play our part to see that His will is fulfilled and His glory revealed in our lives.

It Reveals His Grace:
"Grace is God's Riches at Christ's Expense" says Pastor W.F. Kumuyi. God's will on any situation is a product of His grace. This is because *"... of his fullness have all we received, and grace for grace."* John 1: 12. Grace makes you to flourish in God's programme for your life. In effect,

you become unstoppable. You operate at a level that amazes everyone around. One of the greatest impacts of grace is that it perfects your plans and makes your actions result oriented. A good example of a minister who had an unstoppable ministry as a result of grace was Apostle Paul. The more he was imprisoned, the more he seized those opportunities to write seasoned letters that have become books for over one thousand eight hundred (1800) years and he ministered to highly placed individuals that he could not have access to physically. Though he was extensively persecuted, he saturated Asia Minor with the gospel of Christ.

Jeremiah was another prophet whose ministry reflected God's grace. Many times, his prophecies were burnt in order to hinder the fulfillment of the promise God gave him in Jeremiah 1:5. Yet, today, his prophecies are being read all over the world. When he was thrown into the dungeon to die prematurely, he came out miraculously. To confirm that his ministry was dominated by grace, the Babylonian armies were charged to give him freedom while the Israelites were enslaved.

God wants us to position ourselves to maximize His grace in our lives. Mary was favoured to be the mother of Jesus based on grace. However, she positioned herself to be a beneficiary of such an opportunity by accepting the proposal to be married to Joseph. If she rejected Joseph's proposal she would have been disconnected from such a favour. Joseph was a descendant of David, in effect, connected Mary to be the mother of the promised Messiah.

In Luke 12:32 the scripture states that *"Fear not little*

flock; for it is your Father's good pleasure to give you the Kingdom." I learnt of a woman who was at the point of death yet utilized the last opportunity she had to cry for God's mercy before crossing to the great beyond. Indeed, she found it. When she got to the place where men were being judged, Jesus appeared with blood flowing all over his body as it was at Calvary, and took the woman to heaven. The prophet who saw the vision wondered why she had such a great privilege. It is because God is ...*not willing that any should perish, but that all should come to repentance.* (2 Peter 3:9). God's will for her to enter heaven was unstoppable due to the fact that God's grace was revealed in her life.

It Reaffirms God's Greatness:
Some people grope in darkness not knowing that their eyes have been blind folded from God's purpose for their lives. It is often said that unspeakable riches are lying in the grave own by those who could not fulfill their destinies.

Fortunately, God revealed the wonder that makes his will unstoppable by crushing Goliath before David, Sennacherib before Hezekiah, Jezebel before Elijah and Herod before Peter. God ensures the fulfillment of His will because it reveals the finality of His greatness.

When Satan appeared in heaven to resist God's will in Revelation twelve, they overcame and cast him out by the blood of the lamb. When he attempted destroying God's will for Peter, Jesus demonstrated the superiority of God's power over his power. And the scene at Christ crucifixion and resurrection attested to the fact that God's will is unstoppable.

If it seems as if God's will concerning certain issues in your lives are delayed, keep your faith alive, pray and systematically take action. God will certainly demonstrate His power because He delights in the accomplishment of His will.

It Reaffirms God's Genuineness:
Why should Joseph be killed by his brothers when he was to fulfill God's promise to Abraham that his seed would be strangers in a strange land? And why should Moses be killed by the mid-wives of Pharaoh when he was to fulfill the second part of God's promise to Abraham that his seed would come out from that land after four hundred (400) years? Though Moses and Joseph faced cruel challenges, God's word stood fast in the end.

God does not want us to be like Zacharias who doubted the possibility of His will concerning Elizabeth's conception. We must not relate with God based on our emotions but by faith. No matter how hopeless a situation may look. The moment God reveals His will, He expects us to be certain of its fulfillment. Remember the click (action) that gave rise to the resurrection of Lazarus was obedience to the directive of Jesus that they should roll away the stone. Immediately they did that, the reality that he had spent four days in the grave became a past tense.

A lot of people like the Scribes, Pharisees and the watchmen who were assigned to watch over the body of Christ at his death must be put to shame in our lives, ministries and families. While our trust in God is tried, the faithfulness He demonstrated in the past testifies that He will forever be truthful to His promises and covenants towards us.

GOD'S WILL IS UNDENIABLE

"...What shall we do to these men for indeed a notable miracle hath been done by them is manifest to all them that dwell in Jerusalem; and we cannot deny it." (Act 4:16)

The wonder of God's operation in every generation has proved that His will is undeniable. The question above emerged due to the manifestation of God's power in the name and resurrection of Christ Jesus. The Sadducees who were resisting the Lordship of Christ were amazed at the possibility of the power in his name as it brought healing to a man of forty (40) years that was born lame.

The book of Daniel for instance shows an undeniable connection between Daniel's vision and the change in world power. When God was to overthrow Babylonian empire, Belshazzar the fifth king who reigned after Nebuchadnezzar saw hand writing on the wall while he drank with the vessel of God's temple. The interpretation Daniel gave to the hand writing the king saw was *"... MENE; God hath numbered thy kingdom, and finished it. TEKEL; Thou art weighed in the balances, and hath found wanting. PERES; Thy kingdom is divided, and given to the Medes and Persian..." in that night was Belshazzar the king of the Chaldeans' slain, and Darius the Median took the kingdom.* (Dan 5: 26-28, 30-31): Power was transferred from Darius of Medes to Cyrus of Persia to Alexander the Grecian until it got to the Roman Empire. This has produced forty-seven (47) modern day nations, and they will all give way for Christ's millennial reign.

Most people deny the will of God secularly and ministerially for the following reasons:

1. Underestimation: This was the experience of Christ with the Galileans. They felt they knew all about his destiny because they knew the status of his family. They missed the blessings of his ministry due to underestimation.

If God has purposed that you will accomplish greater feat than your predecessors, keep looking unto Jesus, never allow negative attitudes from yourself and others to bind the purpose of God for your life. The fact that you are not yet a known authority in God's purpose does not mean you will not be successful. Be it in our spiritual pursuit, business, educational career, ministry, marriage and the like. God has promised that we will be the head.

Therefore, any step taken in line with God's will for our lives should be with optimism because it packages surprises, amidst challenges. Negative attitude has ruined the destiny of many. But as long as you believe in the God of all possibilities, move forward, you will soon be a wonder to those who are denying God's purpose for your life.

Remember, the churches in the days of John Wesley and White Field denied the call of God on their lives. Fortunately, White Field started open air programme (crusade) and was the first person to gather ten thousand (10 000) people in an outdoor Christian gathering. And the exploit of John Wesley's ministry superseded those who denied God's call upon his lives.

2. Self Seeking: God wants us to be careful in the way we relate with people around us. God does not give consideration to personal opinion before He chooses any one to fulfill any purpose. He chose seemingly insignificant children like Samuel, David and Esther. So far, most peoples' attitude towards such individuals has not been encouraging. If you notice God's grace or His hand on any individual, you are expected to join the likes of Aquila and Priscilla who expounded the knowledge of Apollo in Christ and made him more relevant to the Corinthians church. Some people ignore God's call on others because they feel they do not match their expectation. That is self in action. Historic event has proved that God's will is by grace. Most Jews at Jerusalem did not acknowledge the ministry of Paul yet, he was taken to Heaven, wrote fourteen books in the New Testament, established vibrant churches, raised remarkable leaders and saturated the then world with the gospel. This proves that man may decide to deny God's will in a situation but God will definitely confirm His will in His children if they can pray.

3. Ignorance: This was the reason why Christ lamented in Luke 19:41-42 "...when he was come near, he beheld the city (Jerusalem), and wept over it, Saying if thou hadst known...in this thy day, the things which belong unto thy peace! But now (as a result of ignorance) they are hid from thine eyes". The ignorant proudly despise God's will with a false confidence that all is well. Such was the case of the Israelites who rejected the hour of their visitation because they felt Christ was not the Messiah but a blasphemer. We must endeavour to get rid of ignorance in our relationship with God by seeking His guidance and mercy always. It is a pity that ignorance does change God's will but hinders the ignorant from being a beneficiary of His will.

GOD'S WILL IS IRRESISTIBLE

Joshua was called by God to lead God's people to the promise land. The enemy nations were more recognized and outnumbered his army, still, he triumphed. The push of the kings of the Amorites against Joshua did not stop Israel from possessing her possession. The haters of Christ appointed soldiers to secure his sepulcher, in order, to hinder the prophetic fulfillment of Christ resurrection. In the end, He resurrected in the presence of the soldiers. If God reveals His will to you, count yourself privilege, do not doubt Him neither should you allow anything to give you option B. Others might have failed in your present pursuit, ensure patience as you press forward with the assurance of the possibility in God's presence which guarantees assistance, because He has promised that "...*I will strengthen thee; yea, I will help thee...*" (Isaiah 41:10b).

God's will for Jacob when He instructed him to return to his father's house was that His presence will be with him. Unfortunately, Esau decided to come against him with 400 men. The thought of Esau and his army on their way to attack propelled him to engage in consistent fervent prayers. Thank God he prevailed and a supernatural operation was carried out on Esau which changed his intention immediately he saw Jacob. His hardened heart was broken and instead of killing Jacob, he kissed him.

The bottom line is that God's will for Jacob to return to His father's house was fulfilled.

WAYS OF RESISTING RESISTANCE TO GOD'S WILL FOR YOUR LIFE

1. Remember God's Faithfulness
2. Exercise Faith
3. Pray
4. Speak Positively

1. Remember God's Faithfulness: The thought of God's faithfulness reduces pressure. Definitely, God has done spectacular things in your life or in the lives of those around you. Reflect and refresh your mind on them and you will not magnify any challenge on your way to God's will for your life.

2. Exercise Faith: An unshakable trust in God's covenant promises and power inspires you and provides new strength and zeal to triumphantly press into the reality of God's will for your life.

3. Pray: Tough situation requires tough prayer. The mistake made by most people is that they run away from challenges. Notwithstanding, it is being said that "tough situations never last but tough people do," prayer is the major channel through which we receive directives that give victory over resistance and paralyze the power that wants to stop us.

4. Speak positively: The same creative power that was

demonstrated through God's word at creation serves as an example for us who were created in His image. Never allow the challenges before you to influence your words negatively. Remain positive.

5. Watch: The Bible warns the believer to watch and pray. Watching makes praying meaningful. Praying without watching makes you a religionist who thinks prayer is the peak of man's relationship with God. Prayer is good but, it is not sufficient without watching.

Watching is the determinant of your closeness and obedience to God. It helps you to discover your wrongs so you can put them right to avoid God's wrath and disapproval of your relationship with Him and service in His Kingdom. A child of God who does not watch would be diverted from God's will. He or she may be loaded with activity but in reality has been swayed from his or her ministerial and God ordained responsibility.

GOD'S WILL IS INCONTESTABLE

History has revealed repeated cases when God's will was brought to a contest. Yet, God has proved himself as the Almighty. Moses came into a contest with the magicians of Egypt to fulfill God's will of delivering Israel. Elijah entered a contest with the prophets of Baal to restore Israel. Aaron faced a contest with the Levites to maintain his position as the priest. Each of them came out victorious because they were fulfilling the will of God for their lives. God's will is incontestable. None of those people who challenged the authority of God's will were able to win because contesting with God's will either in the life of a child of God, a church or in a nation is a waste of time and effort.

Every rung of our progress into God's will for our lives holds one form of contest or the other. Some are physical while others are not. Fortunately, if our aspirations originate from God's will for our lives things work for our good.

Pastor W.F Kumuyi went to Russia to minister to students but, the Christian body also requested that he should also minister to them. The condition attached to the ministration was that it must be during the day. This was due to their belief that African ministers use fetish power. The ministration took place at the Upper House where they declared for seventy years that there was no God. While the man of God was ministering, some people went to place a woman that has been paralyzed for twenty-five years at the entrance of the venue. This was to contest and convince people that God does not exist therefore; they should not expect divine recovery for a paralyzed woman.

At the close of the ministration while people were coming out of the venue, the woman rose up and started to walk! No one can contest with God.

If anyone failed to accomplish God's will for his or her live, it is not because the enemy is that powerful but because they failed to play their part or follow God's directives. The worst they can do sometimes is to cause a delay. Delay is never a denial. It pushes you to pray until something happens.

GOD'S WILL IS UNQUESTIONABLE

You can question your president about the budget of the

nation but you cannot question God on why he decided to make Joseph the head over his elder brothers. You can question the construction of a building but not why God created some people black and others white.

He may decide to reveal some reasons for certain actions and outcomes if you are His dear servant. Yet, it is not in all things or at all times He replies man's question. Get me right, the will of God for your life is different from the will of Satan or the will of man. If for instance, there is recurrent case of premature death in a particular family. Anyone who is concerned can seek and ask God for the cause in prayer and God will answer. This is because premature death is not His will for our lives. Or if a particular lineage suffers from abject poverty, one of them can seek the face of God to know the reason. In most cases, He gives answer. Why? In Psalm 23 and other books of the scripture, He promised us long life and prosperity. But, you cannot question Him on your gender, why Jesus is the only way to heaven, why He pardoned Manasseh with the gravity of his sin or why He decided to make Peter the head of the early church.

REASONS WHY GOD'S WILL IS UNQUESTIONABLE

1. He is the final authority
2. He knows the end from the beginning
3. He determines Times and Seasons
4. He has perfect knowledge of all things
5. He is a just God
6. He is the Giver of Life
7. He controls all things

1. He is the final Authority: Legitimate authority is

power. It determines the level of one's operation and control. Your level of authority determines the scope of your influence and decision making.

The accusers of Meshach, Shadrach and Abednego could not cast them into the fire except the king himself because he alone had the authority. None could have rewarded Mordecai except the King Ahasuerus. Authority can never be compromised. A little wonder king Uzziah became leprous when he offered incense to God and Saul rejected as king for carrying out a sacrifice that Samuel was supposed to offer.

God is the highest authority. He needs no permission from anyone to take any decision. You must allow the fact that God's will for your life is backed by His superior authority to generate confidence and faith in your mind. This was the secret of Daniel while he was thrown into the Lion's den and Peter when he was imprisoned by Herod. Count yourself fortunate and utilize the opportunity of being a believer. His authority over your lives and destiny defies the works of darkness.

2. He knows the beginning from the end: Why was the ambition of men to build the tower of Babel scattered? It was because God knew that man had sinned and needed cleansing to make it to heaven. More so, He knew that man was to replenish the earth: continue for many generations until the seed of the woman will bruise the head of the serpent as prophesied in Genesis 3: 15.

It seems as if God is not fast enough to put an end to the killing of Christians in the world. You should remember that, Jesus prophesied in Matt 24: 9 *"Then shall they deliver you up to be afflicted, and shall kill you: and ye shall be hated of all nations for my name's sake"*. This means that Jesus knew from the onset that the church at large would face persecution. You may alert the police and the soldiers but the truth is that they can only try their best within the limit of God's help. It is only God that can put an end to an event that was prophesied by Jesus.

3. He determines Times and Seasons: Nothing takes God unaware even the plans of Satan are at His fingertips because there is no darkness before Him.

Think of Joseph who thought it was over. First, he was sold as a slave and to worsen the situation, he was imprisoned. He remained in prison for over two years. The natural man would have thought God's will for his life will never come to pass any longer. God showed who He is and caused Joseph to come at His own time to fulfill God's purpose for his life.

I learnt of a man who was a missionary in his church. The senior pastor called him from the missionary field for no reason. He was told to spend some moments in prayer. Months passed until a year was over; He spent six years praying. He became an ordinary member in the church, until one day things turned round and he was called back to be a state leader in that church.

Have you forgotten about Sarah? She gave birth to Isaac at 89 years, Elizabeth gave birth to John at old age; Mary also gave birth to Jesus after fifty-two generation of earnest expectations of the Israelites.

Many Christians get into unnecessary stress and anxiety when they try to determine the timing of God's purpose for their lives for God. All that was expected of Saul to maintain his position as the king of Israel was to wait for Samuel to offer sacrifice. He waited till the morning of the seventh day and gave up waiting. I pray that every power that wants you to give up before your dream comes through will be destroyed in Jesus name.

If Saul was asked to pay a material price for his victory he would have gone all out to get it, but all God wanted from him was the price of character and he failed. We must take our heart to the cross and ensure that we daily work on our character so it does not betray us. Your ability to wait for God's timing for your life shows your level of maturity.

REASONS WHY PEOPLE DO NOT WAIT FOR GOD'S TIMING

- Fear
- Wrong counsel
- Impatience
- Inaccurate assumptions
- Overconfidence

You need to do a realistic check of your life. A discovery of any of these negative characters should be addressed with all seriousness. They stand as enemies to God's timing for your life.

4. He has perfect knowledge of all things: A colleague of mine narrated her experience to me when she was to get married. She said that she consecrated her body to God and determined that she will get married to a Christian. During her National Youth Service, many people came to ask her hand in marriage but she refused. The one that surprised me is a man she said kept coming and did not give her time to pray about it. Today, he would invite her to evangelism and tomorrow another church programme. Thank God she rejected all his invitations. One day, God showed her who the man was. She saw herself in a dream in a village inside a hurt and the man who brought her left her and went drinking under a palm tree. The dream gave her serious concern because this man was still disturbing her.

One day as she went to her mother in the Lord and narrated her experiences the woman told her that the man is not God's will for her marriage. Meanwhile, when the woman first saw her, the first thing she did was to congratulate her for finding the will of God for her life in marriage. After she discussed the purpose of her visitation, the woman said that God revealed to her that there is a man who approached her and she has not given him reply. It was then she remembered when the man she married approached her. She did not pray about it but told him to give her time to pray, but her delay made the man to give up. She said that at a point, God asked her why she kept the man waiting without giving him a reply. Due to the fact that he came for NYSC, she did not see him again, except the other man.
When she was through with her with National Youth Service, she went back home and surprisingly, the man that God revealed to be a deceiver came to her house.

While he introduced the topic of marriage, she was told that she has a call on her landlord's landline. It was the man that has been waiting for her reply. She wondered how he got her landlord's number. After their discussion, she went back to the other man and opened up to him that he was a deceiver pretending to be a believer. She went further to telling him that God has revealed to her that he is a drunkard, on hearing that he went home in shame.

No secret can be hidden from God. He has perfect knowledge of all things. When Samuel was sent to anoint one of the children of Jesse, no one knew why He told Samuel not to anoint Eliab but David. Until, we got to 1Samuel 17, when Goliath threatened Saul and the armies of Israel Eliab whom Samuel intended to anoint was there and could not stand. God already had knowledge of how he would respond to challenges. Therefore, He chose David. Though David did not have the approval of men yet he confronted the enemy nation and defended the cause of heaven.

5. He is a just God: - God has never programmed evil for His children. Whenever a child of God faces situations like delay in childbearing, unemployment, sickness, failure and so on, the believer is supposed to check his or her life to ensure that sin is not present. After which, he or she should take it to the Lord in prayer with the assurance that all things will work together for good.
Imagine our Lord Jesus going through the shameful death on the cross. Quite unpleasant, but immediately he said "*...it is finished...*" (John 19:30) the veil of the temple rent, the rock rent, the mountains rent. The graves

were opened and many saints came out of the grave and appeared to many people in the city. This reveals that though his death was painful, God permitted it because it was His will and it served an indispensable purpose to man.

The question is, if God revealed a future occurrence of the programme of the wicked aimed at causing you, your loved ones or neighbours arm; If you fail to pray seriously or possibly fast to destroy such agenda of the wicked and if eventually such plans came through, you cannot blame God. This is because He expected you to take advantage of the knowledge of future events He gave you to counter the enemy.

Chapter Four

FIND OUT GOD'S WILL FOR YOUR LIFE

Matthew 7:7 *"…seek, and ye shall find…"*

We invest a lot of money to seek the best doctors, counselors, business idea and so on but the average man hardly spent time to search for God's will. Many people are not living in the blueprint of God's will for their lives. They completely rely on chance to pave a way for them. All they concentrate on is to acquire a good car, house, job and others. These things are part of God's will for our lives but God's will is beyond materialism. Moses was faced with the challenge of choosing between the will of God for his life and the position of leadership in Egypt. God's will is that purpose that makes your life count for eternity. It may be in marriage, academic pursuit, place of residence, ministry, place of worship etc. It remains the only pursuit that will give joy, unlimited satisfaction and eternal reward.

You must give attention to the word SEEK to facilitate the discovery of God's will for your life. The fact that the word "SEEK" is an action word shows the place of action oriented drive in finding out God's will for your life. The disappointment that accompanies the failure and problems that one experience when steps are taken and decisions made either due to people's advice or personal intention, make seeking God's will inevitable.

How can I find out God's will for my life?

(1) LOOK INSIDE (Meditate):

"For as he thinketh in his heart so is he..." (Prov 23:7) Your real person lies in your spirit that is deep within you. You can only connect with all the glorious things that God has packaged in your life when you look inside. God's will is not far away from you. It is as close as your deepest thoughts. Whatever you are trying to find out in God, your thought remains the gate. It makes up your passion: passion make up your decision; decision action and action destination.

Thought >> Passion>> Decision>> Action>> Destination.

God's will influence your life and that of others around you positively. It is void of selfish interest and desires.
God's children seek His will in all things. In most cases, it is aimed at building and expanding the kingdom of God. Experience has proven that any thought that is backed up by the scriptures and supported by the Holy Ghost is the will of God. As you look inside, always ask yourself that what am I passionate about? What is calling my attention at the moment, most especially after spending much time in prayer, giving of alms, made efforts to be attentive to God and have ensured consistent obedience to God? If you

are indeed a child of God who has laid all on the altar, one who is not hiding or dragging anything with God, any thought that gives you peace of mind and occupies every part of you, gives a positive insight into what the future holds for you takes you into a new page of God's glory in your life. Being proactive about it is therefore important.

Peace always characterizes any idea that God puts into your heart. It is His desire to perfect that which concerns every area of our lives. Therefore, He makes your conscience to experience peace when you are in His will. Remember the heart of a believer is different from that of a sinner that feels comfortable in sin. In most cases, if the step that you are about to take contradicts God's plan for you at that point in time you will experience intense fear rather than peace. God also sends people your way to counsel you against such steps and confirms His will through dreams or visions. This is because He knows that if you do not understand the reason for such an intense fear, you will understand the counsel of children of God and if that is difficult for you to comprehend, you will understand dreams and visions. Such steps may not be sinful but are not in the center of God's will for your life at the moment. This was what happened to Balaam when he decided to go with the men of Balak, Jehoshaphat intended to go to war with Ahab and the ship that took Saul and other prisoners from Myra to Rome.

At some point in my Christian life, I came in contact with a book written by a great man of God. It was titled "Exploits of Faith". It was an interesting book that greatly blessed my life because I was passing through a moment of great trials which almost weakened my faith. The book helped to revive my faith. The impact of the book got me thinking. I became concerned about another man of God who never wrote such books. He concentrated on evangelism and holiness. Fortunately for me that day, I came across a book written by Pastor Sunday Adelaja titled "Church Shift". While I read that book, I discovered that the concentration of heaven is on the expansion of the kingdom of God and the transformation of sinners. It focused on discipling a whole nation. He gave reasons why we should not only use our faith to acquire wealth but to disciple a whole nation. It opened my eyes to the will of God for my life as a minister of the gospel. I am supposed to be like Jesus in the presentation of the gospel. *"And Jesus went about all the cities and villages, teaching in their synagogues, and preaching the gospel of the kingdom, and healing every sickness and every disease among the people"* (Matthew 9:35).

The focus point should be on the kingdom and evangelism. The God of the kingdom will add prosperity and other things to those who fully follow His will.

Though Christ turned water into wine, provided money for Peter through the fish belly, multiplied bread and fish to feed the multitude, healed a lot of people, he gave priority to preaching; the work of his father. He said *"I must work the work of him that sent me while it is day: the night cometh, when no man can work"* (John 9:4).

The persecution confronting the present day church calls for evangelism that produces genuine salvation experience. For instance, if a church is burnt, houses destroyed and the lives of people are wasted because the persecutors assume that anyone bearing a Christian name or present in a Christian gathering is heaven bound. What will be the faith of such people, considering the fact that many of them deny being a Christian at the point of being killed? This is why preachers should passionately and persistently preach messages of salvation and holiness to save our generation from destruction.

Therefore, thought shapes destiny and takes you into God's will for your life. Watch your thoughts so that your destiny will not be manipulated.

(ii) LEARN FROM OTHERS:

There is nothing that God desires for you that someone else has not experienced or achieved. It may not necessarily be those in your environment. You can find them in literature. Personally, all the books I have read have influenced my life and ministry positively. They all suit my purpose and have sharpened my vision about the will of God for my life. You cannot stop reading neither can you stop learning from others. Get books that will build your spiritual and secular backbone. Your passion and pursuit should be taken seriously while searching for books.

(iii) LISTEN TO INSTRUCTIONS:

"The right words of our elders are words of wisdom"
God's kingdom is blessed with men and women who have wealth of experience and the spirit of discernment. If you sincerely seek counsel from such people, God will use them to minister to you.

(iv)LISTEN TO THE INNER VOICE:
The inner voice has enabled a lot of Christians to discern God's will for their lives. Your inner voice as a child of God cannot deceive you except you try to suppress it with unrealistic assumptions that bring you into a state of confusion. The inner voice never assumes. It speaks based on God's will on an issue. It speaks the mind of God. You may not understand the depth of what is revealed to you through the inner voice but as you obey God, you come into the reality of God's will for your life. The determination to consistently operate under the auspices of the inner voice helps you enjoy maximum benefit from it. It stands as your prophet. Being attentive to it guarantees all round perfection.

The inner voice empowers you to make the right decision, associate with the right set of people, take the right step and give inspired presentation. The stronger your inner voice, the stronger you become, while the weaker your inner voice, the weaker you become. It is difficult for people to deceive you when your inner voice, is alive. Evangelism is made easy; counseling result oriented; prayers direct to the point; secular work enjoys dynamism; leadership vision oriented and child training effective. No child of God should be left out from this experience.

MAXIMISE YOUR INNER VOICE

How wonderful would it have been if everyone in the church in this century has learnt how to maximize the inner voice. The church would have been vibrant; believers triumphant and business ideas would have been in abundance.

To maximize the inner voice;
    a. Be attentive;
    b. Be used to it (differentiate it from other voices);
    c. Avoid unbelief;
    d. Be submissive;
    e. Inform your spouse;
    f. Pray for a clearer illumination;
    g. Act on it;
    h. Give priority to it over other voices;
    i. Wait on God for a deeper comprehension;
    j. Avoid talkativeness;
    k. Confirm it in the light of God's word;
    l. Give God quality praise;
    m. Be patient.

(v) LINK UP HEAVEN:
"Call upon me, and I will answer thee, and show thee great and mighty things, which thou knowest not." (Jer 33:3)
There are times when prayer becomes indispensable while seeking God's will. He has promised to show us great and mighty things. These are mysteries about the church, our families and our personal lives. It helps us to operate in the realm of God's will and word.

Pastor Sunday Adelaja, the overseer of Embassy of God, Ukraine stated in his book "Church Shift" the surprising directive God gave him when his church was faced with a great challenge that threatened the continuation of his ministry. The government of Kjiv where his church is situated informed people that they should not listen to pentecostal preachers. Fortunately, Pastor Sunday's church increased daily despite the resistance from the government. The government also denied him landed property to put up a permanent structure. It was in this condition his church grew to 25 000 members. To worsen the situation, they were not allowed to use a rented apartment for long. They were being moved from one place to another until the government threatened that they do not have any place to let out to them any longer and that the place they occupy presently is to be renovated, so, they should move out of the country.

When the date that was given to them to vacate the apartment got closer, Pastor Sunday decided to seek the face of God in prayer. God told him to protest. He has been fasting for a very long time with the hope that God will touch the government and cause them to behave responsibly to the church but it did not work. Instead, God said His will for them concerning the situation at hand was that they should protest against the government. After some period of reluctance, they carried out the protest. He took 2000 of his members and they embarked on a peaceful protest. To his surprise and that of his members, as soon as he addressed the government through mega phone, the president came out and promised them a land worth $5 million without requesting any amount of money from them. Everyone, including the media was astonished!

Prayer opens up the map of God's programme for your destiny. The steps to be taken become clearer. As you act, each step taken becomes the exact step needed to connect you with God's will for your life.

Chapter Five

A CALL TO SACRIFICE FOR GOD'S WILL

The average man experiences joy at the revelation of God's will. We feel comfortable when it is within our reach but become nervous when it crosses our way and plan. Friend, it is not what you intend doing but what God wants done. This is where sacrifice comes in. It is a pity that many people abandon God's will at this point.

GOD'S WILL REMAINS THE BEST OPTION FOR MAN'S ASPIRATIONS

The challenge to sacrifice for God's will is unavoidable. But when the call comes to you to sacrifice for God's will, remember Hebrew 12:12 *"Looking unto Jesus the author and finisher of our faith; who for the joy that was set before him endured the cross, despising the shame, and is set down at the right hand of the throne of God"*. Without sacrifice, it is sometimes impossible to do God's will. To sacrifice for God's will, implies that you give up something that gives you momentary satisfaction to the Lord.

Hebrews 12:2 makes it clear that joy comes after cross bearing. But the inconveniences that accompany the cross make majority to avoid it.

Why is God's Will the best?

1. It produces result beyond expectation: What would have happened at the arrival of Judas and the multitude that were sent by the high priest, when Peter brought out the sword if Jesus had not smutted to the will of God? ... *Jesus said, unto him, Put up again thy sword into his place, for all they that take the sword shall perish with the sword. Thinkest thou that I cannot now pray to my Father, and he shall presently give me more than twelve legions of angels?* (He understood the place of sacrifice in actualizing God's will. If He failed to sacrifice His comfort and convenience for God's will), *how then will the scriptures be fulfilled, that thus must it be?* (Matt 26:52-54).

Crucifixion was a difficult task yet, Christ endured it for humanity because that was the only way into God's fullness. It brought true righteousness and drew a line between religion and regeneration. The amazing exploits, manful ministers, multiple disciples and miracles that have been in manifestation for over 2000 years till now serve as a pointer to the indispensability of Christ death and the worth of His sacrifice. Most importantly the numbers of people who have accessed heaven since then are innumerable.

What Makes His Death Unique?
Matt 27:50-53 *"Jesus, when he had cried again with a loud voice, yielded up the ghost. And, behold, the veil of the temple was rent in twain from the top to the bottom; and the earth did quake, and the rocks rent; And the graves were opened; and many bodies of the saints which slept arose, And came out of the graves after his resurrection, and went into the city*

and appeared to many" This experience would not have been recorded if He did not sacrifice himself for man.

Being a blessing to the world at the expense of pain requires sacrifice. God never fails, after pain comes gain and strain produces abundant rain.

2. It will maximize His grace in your life: God's will does not centre on your feelings but on the grace of God for your life. Moses felt he could not speak, Jeremiah was a child, Gideon was the youngest in his father's house and they were poor. The list is endless. Yet, God has proved man wrong in this regard. Whenever God's will requires that you face a mountain, you must rest assured that He has given you the grace to surmount that situation.

Gideon never thought he could confront the Midianites not to talk of triumphing over an army of 135000 men with a team of 300 men. While he was hiding, the grace that guarantees Israel's victory was embedded in him. In most cases, we carry the possibility of extraordinary feat in us without our knowledge.

I came in contact with a man of God who was led by the spirit of God to wait on the Lord for 100 days so as to experience deliverance from foundational battles. He thought it was impossible; he fasted for 20 days and stopped. To his surprise the Spirit of God told him that he has not started; He said he must complete the 100 days fasting without interruption. This made the brother to summon courage. This time, he completed the fasting without interruption, and an end came upon his foundational battles. I do not mean that without fasting for 100 days God cannot hear you. That was God's will for him concerning the issue. What matters is that he never thought he could wait on the Lord for 100 days but grace made it possible.

I learnt of another man who was praying for the baptism of the Holy Ghost. At a time, the Spirit of God asked him the amount of time he was spending in prayer and he said one hour, he was asked to increase it and he thought he was ready since he was now spending two hours but he was told to increase it to three and from three to four until he got to eight. He was spending eight hours in prayer! Due to his obedience, he became so powerful to the point that he was made a state leader. Probably he never thought he could pray for eight hours in one day but grace made it possible.

Accessing God's fullness sometimes require a shift that takes you from your comfort zone to a pedestal of sacrificial living. Be ready to be stretched if you are passionate about being used of God. The grace you were given at salvation should be maximized. It is at this point you become transformed into the fullness of the stature of Christ. Most Christians see you as being an extremist whenever you pursue a greater objective in Christ Jesus. In business, holiness, ministry, relationship, giving, family life and secular endeavours we must be ready to sacrifice anything that will probably hinder God's expectation for our lives. Until you meet with God's expectation; you will not come into the reality of true fulfillment.

3. It puts a smile on the face of others: We never can tell how many people will be blessed, empowered and delivered when we despise challenges and sacrificially submit ourselves to God's will. It opens the page of God's plan for our lives and for humanity.

People who sacrificially put smile on the faces of others.
Onesiphorus: - *"This thou knowest, that all they which are in Asia be turned away from me; ... The Lord give mercy unto the house of Onesiphorus, for he oft refreshed me, and was not ashamed of my chain... and in how many things he ministered unto me at Ephesus thou knowest..."* (2 Tim 1:15-18) KJV. Unlike many Christians, Onesiphorus showed an exemplary attribute in giving. His disposition while giving made a difference. Today, many people's benevolence goes along with pride, self-promotion and announcement but his was borne out of love and he did it wholeheartedly. It was not in a reproachful manner. While others abandoned apostle Paul when he was imprisoned. He carefully sought and cared for him. The reverse is the case in many assemblies today: they prefer to relate with the rich and despise the needy. They make children of God who are yet to experience prosperity feel as if they are sinners or not qualified to be in God's presence. We must learn to give to Christians and sinners alike as Onesiphorus did.

Stephanas: You must expect Christ call to a greater height in your Christian pursuit and be ready to operate above the level of the average Christian, where God's glory is revealed in its fullness. The heavier the cross becomes, the greater His hand comes on you. This was the challenge Jesus threw at Peter in John 21:15. Sacrifice is demanded when God requires total commitment to salvation of sinners. It means your visions, ambitions, passion and concentration should major on the salvation of souls. You are not to worry about your needs. God will definitely make provision as you cast your cares on Him and follow the guidance of the Holy Spirit. This is why Peter said in Act 6:4 that *"…we will give ourselves to prayer and to the ministry of the word."* and the supernatural manifestations of God's power, irresistible impart on souls, demonstration of diverse gifts and the operation of the power of resurrection followed that decision.

This was the picture of Stephanas' commitment to the ministry. Neither Jesus nor Paul upbraided him before he saw the need for consecration. Interestingly, his family members were involved in his devotion to God's work. 1 Corinthians 16:15 gives record of their sacrificial service and the resultant effect on Paul. It states that *"I beseech you, brethren, (ye know the house of Stephanas, that it is the first fruits of Achaia, and that they have addicted themselves to the ministry of the saints.)"* Paul also commented in verse 17 that *"I am glad of the coming of Stephanas and Fortunatus and Achaicus: for that which was lacking on your part they have supplied."* The consecration of Stephanas brought joy to Paul. God expects each of us to surrender our lives on the altar of His call so that the world around us will experience joy like in the days of Philip in Samaria.

Mary Slessor: You cannot talk about those who sacrificed for God's will without mentioning a woman like Mary Slessor. She was selfless in her pursuit of God's will and went the extra mile to put a smile on people's faces. She was a Scottish who was born on 2 nd December 1888 and died on 13th January 1915, at age 27. She took the challenge to follow the steps of David Livingstone after his death. Unlike most Christian ladies that would rather bury themselves in the issue of marriage immediately they become twenty years. She applied to the Foreign Mission Board of the United Presbyterian church. After training in Edinburgh, Mary set sail in the S.S, Ethiopia on 5th August, 1876 and arrived at her destination in West Africa. She was sent to Calabar region. Though witchcraft, superstition and sacrifice of twins were prevalent, she remained courageous and continued the work of God.

Her determination led to the deliverance of hundreds of twins who were left in the forest to starve to death or be eaten by wild animals. More so, she prevented the possibility of hundreds of war, healed the sick, stopped the act of making suspects to drink poison.
In August 1888, she traveled north to Okoyong, an area where missionaries were previously killed with the belief that she will not be killed. She lived in Okoyong all the rest of her life (15 years).

She was honoured in Britain as the "White queen of Okoyong." She continued her good works and introduced western education. In 1892, she was made the vice-consul in Okoyong, presiding over the native court and in 1905, she was named Vice-president of Ikot Obong native court. In 1913, she was awarded the Order of St. John of Jerusalem. She was the driving force behind the Hope Waddell Institute in Calabar where Africans learnt different vocations.

Your determination to sacrifice for God's will gives a bountiful result of the revelation of God's nature in the world, contagious joy and unlimited fulfillment. The greatest of all is that you enjoy an eternity of bliss in heaven.

THE PERFECT PICTURE OF AN OUTSTANDING SACRIFICE

Let this mind be you, which was also in Christ Jesus: Who, being found in fashion as a man humbled himself, and became obedient unto death, even the death of the cross. (Heb 2:5a,8). This was the sacrifice that changed history, changed the date of the world, gave birth to heroes that influenced generations, delivered uncountable prisoners and gave humanity the hope of a blissful eternity.

The worth of Christ sacrifice cannot be quantified. He left comfort, glory and an authority that is indescribable for a world full of pain, regrets and inconveniencies for our sake. He was also rejected by the Israelites, afflicted with hunger, confronted with hatred and above all, condemned and crucified.

He shed His blood for our redemption. He prayed for our sanctification and opened the gate into the fullness of the manifestation of the God-head to man. His was an unusual sacrifice and it deserved all reverence and honour through all ages.

Chapter Six

THE KEYS INTO GOD'S WILL

True fulfillment is guaranteed after revelation and comprehension of God's will. Knowledge is power. It empowers you to make the right decision and take the right action at every interval in your pursuit of God's will. Below are keys that unlock the door into God's will:

1. The Key of Knowledge:

Hosea 4:6a *"My people are destroyed for lack of knowledge."* John Wesley was a great evangelist whose exploit for the Lord can never be forgotten but his marriage almost affected his ministry. He married a woman who was not in line with God's plan for his ministry. What he lacked was the knowledge of God's will for his marriage. Knowledge is the key into God's will in any area of your life. We make great mistakes when we do not give priority to God's will in every area of our lives. Your drive towards perfection should propel a desperate desire to know and do His will in all things and at all times.

Our relationship with God enables us to receive revelations and directives that differentiate His will from man's will. There are occasions when God keeps quiet to know if we will seek His face for His will or not. At such an instance, if you see it as a test and quickly seek His face, great. But if not, you may experience pain, if you go ahead of Him.

Hezekiah had such experience. In Isaiah 39:1-6 *"AT THAT time Merodach Baladan, the son of Baladan, King of Babylon, sent letters and a present to Hezekiah; for he had heard that he had been sick, and was recovered. And Hezekiah was glad at them, and showed them the house of his precious things, the silver, and the gold, and the spices, and the precious ointment, and all, that was found in his treasures: there was nothing in his house, in all his dominion, that Hezekiah showed them not. Then came Isaiah the prophet unto king Hezekiah, and said unto him, What saw these men? And from whence came they unto thee? And Hezekiah said, They came from a far country unto me, even from Babylon. Then said he, What have they in thine house? And Hezekiah answered, All that is in my house have we seen: There is nothing in my treasures that I have not shown them. Then said Isaiah to Hezekiah, Hear the word of the LORD of hosts: Behold, the days come that all that is in thine house, and that which thy fathers have laid up in store until this day, shall be carried to Babylon: nothing shall be left, saith the LORD"*

Hezekiah went beyond the appreciation that the king deserve to show them everything he has achieved contrary to God's will.

This is why I counsel people not to reveal everything that God has revealed concerning their future, except to their spouse, prayer partner or mature Christian leaders. This will enable them to support in prayer. You do not know who desires the best for you. Therefore, be watchful as regards who you discuss sensitive issues of your life and family with. It helps us to avoid a lot of problems that arise due to envy. We have people who do not have any vision or dream for their future. Such may not be comfortable when you reveal to them that God has given you revelations that guarantee a bright future.

This proves that God's will is all encompassing. We must open our mind to discern God's will for our lives in every situation as we share the testimony of His goodness with others.

2. The Key of Obedience:

Aspirants of God's will are people with absolute obedience. They wholeheartedly follow the systematic leading of the Holy Spirit. They do not allow present situations to determine their obedience to God.

This was the distinguishing factor in the lives of people like David, Elijah, Moses, Peter and Esther. They accessed the miraculous in their generation. They became the epitome of unusual possibilities. They stood for God's will at the expense of their lives and convenience.

As a result of obedience, Peter had a net breaking miracle from the river where he toiled and caught nothing, the walls of Jericho fell down, the red sea opened, the disciples were transformed to extraordinary and unstoppable ministers, the bible was written, and so on. God is not yet through with man. He still has a lot to accomplish in our lives and the world at large. Disobedience stands as hindrance to the move of His Spirit in our lives. It was God's will to establish Saul's kingdom but disobedience robbed him and his descendants of their destiny. I pray that disobedience will not rob you of your destiny in Jesus' name Amen. 1Samuel 15:22b-23 says *"...to obey is better than sacrifice, and to hearken than the fat of rams. For rebellion is as the sin of witchcraft, and stubbornness is as iniquity and idolatry..."* As you earnestly desire all round fulfillment of God's will for your live, be conscious of an unseen eyes watching your level of obedience to instruction giving either by the Holy Spirit or people whom God sometimes use to communicate with you. A good example is your spouse, pastor and your parents. Your obedience to parent should not break your marriage, rather, it should propel the manifestation of God's blessing and love in your family.

Complete obedience requires that you wait for God's timing in every pursuit or endeavour. By the help of His Spirit, He will make you aware of His timing in every step you intend to take. Joseph waited and David also. They did not allow their passion for their dream to lead to rash actions.

3. The Key of Courage:

God's will comes in different levels. First, it is revealed or discerned, secondly, it is accomplished and thirdly, it is sustained. Courage is what takes you from God's revealed will to its fulfillment. It also gives you the enablement to sustain it. You need courage because the devil always challenges God's will to rob man of his blessings. That was the reason God told Joshua in Joshua 1:7a to"*... be ... strong and very courageous...*"

The Place of Courage in God's Will;
Luke 18:1
You will definitely come across situations that would test and resist your faith on God's revealed will. Joshua never knew all the strategies that will lead to Israel's victory neither did he have insight into how God intended to fight for Israel, yet God told him that the first thing is not strategy but to be strong! This means he must be:

S- Stable and Steadfast,
T- Temperate and Trustworthy,
R- Righteous and Rugged,
O- Obedient and Orderly,
N- Never give up.
G- Graciously influence others.
A little wonder he was able to keep to God's dictate from the beginning till the end of his ministry.

The Exemplary Courage of Jesus
Jesus is the author and finisher of our faith. A close look into how He demonstrated courage in ministry positions us to drive into the fullness of God's will for our lives. Christ courage reveals the following.

(a). It was a product of the Spirit: *Luke 4:14-15 "And Jesus returned in the power of the Spirit into Galilee: and there went out a fame of him through all the region roundabout".* We must be spirit driven to access an irresistible courage that overflows us with an inner force and power that makes us unstoppable in the fulfillment of God's will for our lives.

(b) It was a product of God's choice for Christ's pursuit: *"Luke 4:17-18 And there was delivered unto him the book of the prophet Esaias. And when he had opened the book, he found the place where it was written, The Spirit of the Lord is upon me, because he hath anointed me to preach the gospel to the poor: he hath sent me to heal the brokenhearted, to preach deliverance to the captives, and recovering of sight to the blind, to set at liberty them that are bruised."* When your action is originated from God's direction, it facilitates a kind of courage that accomplishes possibilities amidst impossibilities. You must ensure that you are not like Balaam who went headlong into a journey that ended in his destruction due to the fact that it was not God's choice for his life. He made himself a friend to a man who was fighting against God's people and in the end gave him an idea that led to the death of over 23, 000 Israelites in Moab.

(c) Christ knew His position, power and possibilities in God: *"Luke 5:21-24 And the scribes and the Pharisees began to reason, saying, who is this which speaketh blasphemies? But when Jesus perceived their thoughts, he answering said unto them, What reason you in your hearts? Whether is easier, to say, Thy sins be forgiven thee; or to say, Rise up and walk? But that ye may know that the son of man hath power* *upon earth..."*

Christ's knowledge of God's power in His life gave Him extraordinary courage. We must be certain of God's power in us. Christ said *"...I give unto you power over all the power of the enemy..."* pursue God's will with the Knowledge that you are empowered. It produces in you sufficient grace to walk on the sea of life's troubles until you reach the destiny of God's will for your life. In addition to Christ knowledge of His power in God, He also knew his position in God. This knowledge gave Him victory over all the opposition of Satan that stood as obstruction to God's will for His life. It also impacted unusual courage that made it easy for Him to handle every difficulty on His way to fulfilling His purpose.

Every true Christian has a divine position in Christ that places them above principalities and power. This position was revealed in Eph 2:6 that Christ *"...hath raised us up together, and made us sit together in heavenly places in Christ Jesus."* The revelation of the believer's new position in Christ produces extraordinary courage that subdues kingdoms and facilitates the fulfillment of God's will for our lives. Eph 1:10 says *"... what is the exceeding greatness of his power to us ward who believe, according to the working of his mighty power, which he wrought in Christ, when he raised him from the dead, and set him at his own right hand in the heavenly places, far above all principality and power, and might, and dominion, and every name that is named, not only in this world, but also in that which is to come."* This is the position we occupy as a result of the promotion that redemption has given us. It is a position where you have the opportunity to explore Christ fullness.

This knowledge makes it easy to soar in supernatural courage. The truth about this position is that the kingdom of darkness recognizes and dreads believers who operate from that platform. Such was the confession of the demon in the insane person who molested the seven sons of Sceva about Paul's stand in Christ.

(d) He was certain of solutions to the challenges before His ministry: *John :5-6 "...Jesus... lifted up his eyes, and saw a great company come unto him, he saith unto Philip, Whence shall we buy bread, that these may eat? ...this he said to prove him: for he himself knew what he would do."* Calling and empowerment goes together as God's will while divine provision and required potential goes together. One who is certain of divine provision and the availability of required potential needed for the fulfillment of the will of God for his or her life acts with a greater level of confidence and certainty of unlimited possibilities. This confidence is not a product of pride; it is originated from a strong conviction founded on God's faithfulness. A lot of people run away from doing God's will as a result of the challenges that awaits them on their part to doing God's will.

The verse of the scripture that was considered above reveals the level of divine revelation of solution to the ministerial challenges that accompanied the ministry of Jesus. This solution oriented insight fortified Him to face out the challenges before His calling. Was His certainty of the solution ahead of His ministry limited to miracles? No. In John 10:14,15b, 18 *"He said I am the good Shepherd, and know my sheep, and am known of mine...I lay down my life for the sheep...No man taketh it from me, but I lay it down of myself. I have power to lay it down, and I have power to take it again. This commandment have I received of my Father."* He did not approach crucifixion in fear, but, with assurance of God's command (word) concerning His death. God's word provided a ready solution to the challenge of fear and disobedience to God's will for His death on the cross. God has provided solutions to the challenges that will come our way in life and ministry in His word.

Your knowledge of the solutions that God has reserved for you as you give quality time to the study of His word while advancing to do His will strengthens your faith in the Lord. One of such words that give us courage is found in Eph 3:20 God *"...is able to do exceeding abundantly above all that we ask or think, according to the power that worketh in us,".* Although there are occasions when God gives revelations or prophetic solutions to the challenge that awaits us on our way to doing His will. The account of the scripture above is a great privilege that will suffice us in any circumstances we find ourselves. This verse provides solution to financial, marital, national, ministerial and organizational challenges. It opens our eyes to the unlimited power of God and total support as we walk in His will.

Channels of Activating Christ's Courage
We need to activate Christ's exemplary courage. This will help us to accomplish all that God has packaged for us on earth. In order to activate the exemplary courage of Christ, we must do the following:

- Continue in prayer Acts 2 1:14.
- Be filled with the Holy Ghost Acts 2:1-4
- Live in the consciousness of God's presence. Josh 1:9
- Be obedient to God's command. Josh1:9a
- Retain the fire of the word. Jeremiah 20:9
- See into the supernatural Act7:52-56
- Defend God's will. Acts 26:12:19
- Do not be ashamed of God's will. Rom 1:16
- Have faith in God's power amidst confrontation. 1Kings 19:7-13
- Focus on finishing well. 1Kings 19:14-17

4. The Key of Prayer:

Prayer holds the key to the revelation of God's fullness for your life and victory over every form of stumbling block we may come across. If you are fortunate to receive the grace for a greater purpose in your family, it should increase your prayer life. Uneasy lies the head that wears the crown. Do not make the mistake of announcing what God has revealed to you to everyone, rather, pray until it comes to pass. You must be ready to sacrifice sleep and wrestle like Jacob, earnestly seek God until the rain falls like Elijah; continue until answer comes like Daniel, and until your situation changes like Mordecai.

For your prayer to be answered you must know:

1. When to pray;
2. How to pray.

1. When to pray: Prayer is to a believer as oxygen is to man. The believer's life is centered on prayer. A prayer less believer is a powerless believer. You learn to seek God from the point of your conversion. Do not wait until you are confronted with a great challenge before you start to pray. Make it a habit. The frequency of your communion with God determines the level of His leading you enjoy. The Bible counsels us to pray without season. We are to pray until we have the full picture of God's will for our lives and empowered to fulfill and sustain it. This calls for urgent prayer because the journey of a thousand years starts a day. It therefore presupposes that such prayer should commence in earnest. The earnestness of such prayer is dependent on how holy you are in your walk with God.

2. How to Pray: *"… ask in faith, nothing wavering. For he that wavereth is like a wave of the sea driven with the wind and tossed."* You must learn to relate with God in faith because it is the basis of relationship with God. Do not settle for just anything; seek God's face for His best for your life. God does not walk with just anything. He has a perfect programme for your life; therein lies the miraculous. In 1Kings 22:48 *"Jehoshaphat made ships of Tarshish to go to Ophir for gold: but they went not; for the ships were broken at Eziongeber"* What happened here was that Jehoshaphat made ship with Ahab, king of Israel, whose way was not right before God. Therefore God broke the ship. We should show extreme care in every step we take. God takes kin interest in us. Seeking God guarantees accuracy in the decision and action you exhibit.

The Key of Faith
Faith means,
F-Forsaking,

A-All,
I-I
T- Trust,
H-Him.

You must believe that God's will for your life is the best and must be pursued with all your strength and heart. A lot of people make the mistake of doubting and sometimes reject God's will for their lives.
We need to learn how to approach God's will for our lives with faith. It may not carry the perfect picture of our expectations today but as we follow God's leading things begin to fall in line.

Some people give preference to ideas that come to their mind confirming God's mindset on the idea. Their decision is powered by the principles in most motivational books which tell us to have faith in ideas that has not received approval from God. Such will only work if it is in line with God's will. Remember the idea of Abraham to marry Hagai, Balaam to go with Balak, Isaac to go down to Egypt during the time of famine did not receive the approval of God. Ideas are wonderful if it is inspired by the spirit of God. An idea that makes you extremely afraid and leads to questionable dreams are signs that something may be wrong with it.

You must go to God in prayer for confirmation of the validity of such ideas. If you receive an affirmation from God despite your feelings, dreams and fears pursue your ideas with passion. Sometimes fear come as a result of uncertainty or spiritual confrontations and manipulation that does not want you achieve God's purpose for your life. But if God continues to warn you of the danger ahead if such steps are taken, humble yourself and put your ideas aside and submit to God's directives. God killed Uzah because he touched the ark when it was about to fall. Think about it. God gives priority to His will than man's actions taken without due consideration of His will. God's will was that the Levites should be sanctified to carry the ark. It should not be kept on an ass or horse. Though the mistake that led to his death was caused by David (a man after God's heart), God did not spare his life when he touched the ark; he was judged.

We must have faith on God's will for our lives because;
1. We are crucified with Christ.
2. God controls the universe,
3. Any step motivated by self leads to ruins,
4. Goodness and mercy follow God's will,
5. It leads to fulfillment.

Your faith on God's will have the potential to activate the supernatural. Abraham's decision to obey God's will brought supernatural provision of a Ram, red sea parted for Israel, the hungry lepers met surplus food at the camp of the Syrians, the mouth of lions were shut for Daniel, the power of fire was silenced for the three Hebrew young men and countless other miracles.
Fear and unbelief deny you a lot of things because every time God reveals His will it promises us a blessing. Though you may not be aware of it at the moment, fear has stolen more blessing from people than armed robbers have done. You must be ready to sacrifice personal satisfaction at the platform of consecration and live a life that positions you for God's commendation.

No one should be confused at this point, it is possible for one to desire something and go ahead and accomplish but at other occasions, God has a way of leading us contrary to our initial plan into His perfect plan. For instance, a student may decide to study a particular course in the university and along the line, he finds himself studying something else. A student may intend to attend a particular university amazingly; he gets admission from another one. Such was the case of Pastor E.A Adeboye. He decided to go for a scholarship programme to further his education abroad. Unfortunately, on the day of his interview, the chairman of the scholarship committee was sleeping while others were asking him questions on Mathematics and he was giving them answers at ease. After others were through, the chairman asked a question outside Mathematics, so, Pastor Adeboye took it as a joke and questioned the relationship of the question to Mathematics interview. In the end, he was not granted the scholarship. On his way out of the interview venue, he met a lecturer who told him that since he was so good at Mathematics, he should not bother to study abroad but should go to University of Lagos. That was where he got saved and started his ministry.

More so, you may desire to marry sister A and God will lead you to sister B. That is where you need to exercise faith. You must understand that the change you have experienced which is beyond your control cannot change God's plan for your life because all things will work together for good to suit God's purpose for your life as long as you are prayerful and consistently obedient.

5. The Key of Patience:

Patience is power while impatience is a great destroyer. It is required to pass God's test and to experience His perfect will for your life. Every Christian must ensure the possession of the virtue of patience for them to overcome the wiles of Satan. God has a wonderful plan for all His children but the majority misses out due to impatience. Most Christians are strong when it comes to fasting, evangelism, interpretation of scripture and other obligations in God's house. Unfortunately, a great number of these people lack patience. They fast but cannot wait for the answer. They are like fast food generation they cannot stand the face of persecution and ridicule. They flee from challenges.

These challenges might be might be meant to develop their spiritual strength. They read about characters like Paul, Jeremiah, Philip and others who suffered and withstood great oppositions to advance the course of Christ but refuse to internalize the life style of these patriarchs. They move from one church to another at the slightest of offense. They are Christians who are seeking for pleasure. Their presence in the church is determined by the comfort they enjoy, the position they hold and class of people in such congregations. They do not dream of the lives of pathfinders who suffered all forms of afflictions to give us today's church. They are not revolutionary inclined.

Without patience, you cannot reach the peak of your potential in God. God is looking for the Paul of today who will not be silenced because of persecutions, David who will not run ahead of God to be King over Israel,

Joseph who will continue in service in the prison until He opens the door of his promotion, Zachariah who will not abandon their responsibility in God's house due to personal challenges.

Whenever you intend to do anything, probably, a wedding ceremony; if your parents, pastor, boss and elders around counsel you to be patient in order to solidify your preparation for family responsibility, do not be emotional except God gives a go ahead. To meet up with family responsibilities you must either be a graduate at least N.C.E level or must have learnt a vocation.

The experiences of two brothers taught me a great lesson on doing God's will in marriage. God's will in the area of marriage requires prioritizing divine guidance in the selection of a life partner rather than materialism and human evaluations on an ideal man or woman.
The first brother, was a called minister of the gospel, whose ministry turned many to righteousness but he walked by sight at the point of marriage. He left the sister God led him to and married the daughter of a rich man. Unfortunately, she had a spirit husband which made it difficult for him to have any intimate relationship with her (as husband and wife). Anytime he forces her, he experiences rash all over his body.

The second case was that of a brother whose marriage ended in a divorce. What was the cause of the divorce? The wife advised him to move to a place that is closer to her place of work. He agreed and relocated though it was an expensive decision. After a period of time, he could not afford the rent of the new apartment, so they divorced. To his surprise, after the divorce, he discovered that the house located in an eyebrow area in Lagos was the property of his wife. If his choice of a life partner was dependent on the woman's money, he was disappointed. He does not have the freedom to marry another woman until the death of the former. This means that he must keep praying until God transforms her; it is that serious.

You see why I advise every single (especially) man to have what to feed their family before going into marriage.
You do not need to wait till you get all the money in the world. All you need to go into marital life is the ability to provide basic needs. You may only encounter problems when you marry a woman who is not ready to build a family but only wants to enjoy without sowing.

Those who patiently follow the guidance of the Holy Spirit in every area of their life will definitely win all their battles like David, experience the dawn of God's purpose for their ministry like Moses, receive the double portion like Elisha, receive angelic visitation like Zachariah and Elizabeth and receive the possibility for a new dimension of fruitfulness at old age like Abraham.
I want to assure you as a servant of the Lord that there is no prayer you have prayed that have not received an answer. There is no labour of love whose reward is not on the way and there is no consecration without a corresponding manifestation of God's power. You only "... *have need of patience that, after ye have done the will of God, ye might receive the promise (blessings)."* (Hebrews 10: 36).

6. The Key of Humility:
I consistently receive revelation of God's calling for my life. And my greatest joy is to see those revelations come to reality. Amazingly, I discovered that humility is the gateway of a prosperous life and ministry. Most ministers have closed the door against their possibility in ministry due to lack of humility. Humility was the key of Elisha's double portion, Philip's influence over the Ethiopian Eunuch, the commissioning of the man that took over from the founder of Salvation Army and Hannah's conception of Samuel. The fact that you are very talented, prospered, anointed and creative does not take the place of humility in your advancement.
Matthew 23:12 says"...*whosoever shall exalt himself shall be abased; and he that shall humble himself shall be exalted*"

Your onward progress on the ladder of greatness requires humility. It opens the door for unusual favour for God's children. God's desire to heal Namaan was delayed until he humbled himself and obeyed the directive of Elisha to dip himself in river Jordan seven times. You may be closing the door of God's blessing for your life by being proud in your relationship with your church leaders, boss, husband, wife, neighbours and friends. God detests pride. Miriam, Nathan, Dothan and Abiran, Uzziah all received punishment for being proud.

a. Humility in Marriage: God desires that the marriage of His children should be characterized with peace, friendship, fruitfulness and progress. But some people are not enjoying their marriages because the factors that make marriage to work are missing. One of such factors is humility. It makes your marriage blissful. It puts out malice, argument, self and abusive languages. Indeed, love goes a long way in marriage. Yet, humility increases the flow of love in the family. If the couple argues over any decision to be taken and none of them sees the need to submit to the other, love will fade away from that family while and sadness, malice and hatred will become the order of the day in the marriage. Definitely, we must have sufficient grace to endure unpleasant situations in such marriage. However, that is not the will of God for our marriage.If we do our homework, our marriage blossoms with love, joy, peace and unusual unity

The only limitation to our submission is in the case of sinful desire or suggestion from either party. Whenever either party is requesting something sinful like drunkenness, idolatry, indecent dressing, deceit and any contradiction to God's will for our lives and ministry, we must quickly commence serious prayer if possible with fasting for the other partner so the devil does not ruin our union. If Sapphira had not submitted to Ananias to be deceitful, her life would have been prolonged. But she died prematurely.

I learnt of a woman who told her husband that she has gotten to the peak of the number of children she desires in her marriage therefore, she would not be available for any moment of pleasure with her husband. The man could not seek God's intervention, he went ahead and married another woman. I know it is difficult to do without this aspect of marriage but he should have submitted to God's will for believers in marriage as it is in 1Cor 7:10 *"And unto the married I command, yet not I, but the lord, Let not the wife depart from the husband: But if she depart, let her remain unmarried, or be reconciled to*

her husband: and let not the husband put away his wife."
And at the same time pray against the spirit behind such
decision in his wife.

Believers must watch against the wiles of the devil in
their relationship with their spouses. The devil should
not take advantage of either party due to one weakness or
the other. The husband is in the best position to defend
the marriage by managing and enduring the weakness
of the wife and the wife is in the right position to
defend the marriage by watching over her husband. We
must remember that if we harden our heart towards our
spouse and allow the devil to have his way, we will pay
for the consequences. I believe that if we take time to seek
God in prayer while we make an effort to work towards
the success of our marriage, God will reward our effort
with love, peace and unity in our marriages.

In addition, couples must not allow lack of
understanding to disrupt humility in the family. They
must endeavour to understand themselves. It enables
them to give perfect interpretation to the behaviour of
the other party and reduces the possibility of conflict in
the family. If not, we would be fighting against God's
will for our families. Understanding goes a long way to
establish love and humility in the family. You may find
it difficult to understand the action of your spouse most
especially the wife, except you patiently meditate on the
intention and importance of such actions.

Joseph for instance, thought of sending his wife, Mary
away when he discovered she was pregnant but, while he
thought over it, God intervened. If he had been impatient,

he would not have been able to hear from God. Therefore, patience and prayerful meditation on certain behaviours in your spouse will give insight to why they exhibit such actions. And it becomes easy for a couple to ensure submission which confirms the presence of humility in our homes.

b. Humility in the Workplace: An employment that is preceded by divine guidance positions us into God's programme for our lives.

Humility in an organization gives priority to organizational standards that is supported with good etiquette. It gives consideration to organizational structure in daily activities. One who submits to authorities in the work place does not render eye service, neither complains nor murmur.

Submission is easy when promotion is constant, salary is increased regularly, allowances are granted as at when due and staff seem to get anything they desire from the organization. But we should understand that God sometimes allows His children to work in unfavourable conditions so as to gain knowledge, skill and discipline.

At other occasions, God can use unfavourable work conditions to test your confession of salvation and spiritual maturity. The fact that God's intention is to give you an expected end should serve as an encouragement when it seems your desired possibility in your work is delayed before God. Your friends in other organizations may be earning more money than you at the moment but when God is through with you, your finances will take a new dimension of supernatural increment. He may decide to move you to another organization or inspire you to set up a business that will turn things around. Though, He sometimes opens your door of promotion when you pass His test of patience and faithfulness as He did for Mordecai.

You may find yourself in a place where your boss does not have much educational experience and you find yourself being the pillar of the organization. Be careful as a child of God not to become proud and callous most especially if your boss is a Christian. God has a way of imparting needed virtues and opportunities into your life through your boss.

You may find yourself setting up an organization like the one you have where laboured. Then, your boss will not be a competitor but a helper to see that your own business thrives.

Although Potiphar sent Joseph to prison, it was through his connection Joseph got to the throne. We must be prayerful in the decisions we take. Rash actions may affect our destiny while we are serving others.

When you gossip about your boss or judge them in things that are not sinful, you may be building a stumbling block before yourself. Always put yourself in their position while complaining of their shortcomings. Remember that one day, you will be a leader and would be faced with some of the challenges with which they are faced with today.

You are free to give suggestions that would proffer solutions to your discovery about their leadership style. If they accept, fine, if not, then, learn from the fact that when you become a leader in the future, you must be open to ideas. Since you now have a new understanding that any leader who is close to counsel loses key subordinates who may not be able to stand the sight of an autocratic leader most especially when their leadership is limiting the potential of the organization and her staff.

This does not mean that when God opens a better door you, should neglect it. It means you operate by divine guidance and ensure that God is taking the lead. Though, you may not be happy with the working conditions in that organization do not allow it to result to bitterness, nagging, arrogance and disobedience in carrying out your obligations as long as they are not sinful. In summary,

- Be Hardworking,
- Avoid repeated mistakes,
- Be hard working,
- Be result oriented,
- Do not backbite about anyone,
- Pray for God's favour,
- Be contented,
- Be patient,
- Be filled with praise.

c. Humility in the Family: The spiritual, physical, financial, social and emotional development of the family is paramount to God. He gives much attention to the family because today's world of 6 billion people is a product of a single family which originated from Adam and later Noah. In fact, the family has been the tool through which God accomplished every exploit, invention and transformation we see in our world today.

Humility is of great importance in the family. The mother, father and children must ensure humility in honour of God's will and word. The wonder that God has planned for your family might elude you if humility is missing in your relationship with family members. Humility gives birth to unity, peaceful co-existence, consistent love, divine connection, fellowship and answered prayers.

Transparency is a key factor of humility. A transparent and exemplary father or mother will find it easier to raise their children.

Tolerance builds togetherness and sustains understanding that enables family members to submit to one another: A family where members are quick to judge one another rather than correct one another's mistakes in love will experience friction which sometimes work against submission.

Humility flows naturally in a family where members respect one another. The father respects and submits to the wife's counsel if hers is better in a particular circumstance. The wife also ensures that she does not despise the position of the man as the head of the family while the children seek for a better way to make their views known whenever there is conflicting desires. Though, parents are not to shift ground when they know that they are training their children in the way of the Lord or when their children are about to make a costly mistake.

Spiritual parents also deserve respect and submission. Anyone who despises, secretly insults, openly disobeys or rejects the counsel of true ministers of God will definitely be punished except such a one repents before it is too late. Any mistake discovered in leadership style is not a tool for backbiting but a prayer point to intercede on, most especially when it has nothing to do with sin.

d. Humility in our Studies: I learnt of a lecturer who repeated a topic for several weeks when his students where to write their final exam. Fortunately, only two of them were able to discover that they needed to pay attention to that topic while preparing for their exam. Others took it lightly. Until they got to the exam hall and found that the question was compulsory. They began to lament but the two that paid attention saw it as an opportunity. One of them said that he made use of three pages to answer the question. Many students fail as a result of pride. They disturb while the lecture is on and miss out vital information. Many behave arrogantly and threaten their lecturers when they are called to order.

Many of them in this category believe that the more disrespectful, impolite, disobedient and unconcern you are to lecturers, the more respect you earn. But, many end up as failures in life.
Submission to teachers does not mean giving bribe for examination malpractices. It seemly means respecting your lecturer and behaving yourself responsibly.

e. Humility in your Relationship with Others: You do not know when God will connect you with your divine helpers. Your behaviour will either connect or disconnect you from divine helpers.

Your attitude should not be influenced by the possession of such an individual, but should be based on God's love and His will for us in our relationship with others. Make it a priority to treat others well and be humble. God will reward your actions with divine connection.

I learnt of a security man who did his work with love and courtesy. Others misbehave and fail to understand that their place of work at present is a stepping stone to greater heights. They made pride, disrespect and arrogance the order of the day. As for this security man, he did the work with all his heart. One day, the parent of the children he has related with love and humility took him from where he was to a bigger and better organization. A little wonder the Bible counsels the believers that "...ye younger, submit yourselves to the elder. Yea, all of you be subject one to another, and be clothed with humility: for God resisteth the proud, and giveth grace to the humble." (1 Peter 5:5)

7. The key of Forgiveness:
The focus point of this book is to connect you with the fullness of God's will and wonder for your life. This is what money cannot buy neither can be attained by societal and professional attainment. It can only be accessible through the instrumentality of God's grace.

God as in the Bible days requires holiness from His children whenever He wants to accomplish an extraordinary feat in their lives and family. This implies that you must be spotless and passionate about God's love and will in every area of your life.

It is God's will to answer our prayers at all times even though there are moments that we must patiently wait for God's timing. Unforgiving spirit must be done away with. We must ensure that our heart is free from every offense.

Couples must come to the point when they accept their spouses with their imperfections. The only way to accept your spouse with his/her imperfections is to learn how to forgive. At most, you should bring it to their knowledge. You must not abhor grudges against your spouse or anyone that have offended you. If you do, your access into the miraculous will be blocked. Moreover, Satan can also gain ground in your life.

8. The key of service: - *"If any man serve me, let him follow me; and where I am, there shall also my servant be: If any man serve me, him will my father honour."* (John 12: 26) Honour is God's will for your life, but, majority delight to be honoured by God without the willingness to serve God. Your drive into an honorable life should propel an acceptable and consistent service in you.

How can I serve God?
1. Serve in Truth: John 4:24 *"God is a Spirit: and they that worship him must worship him in spirit and in truth."* Your service of fellowship with God and usefulness in His kingdom must be void of hidden sin and falsehood.
Satan uses hidden sin to rob us of our blessings, which was his intention in the life of a little boy. He was the eleventh son of his father. His mother gave birth to him after much waiting. Interestingly, the child came

after she told her husband "...*Give me children, or else I die*."(Genesis 30:1b) He was the love of his father who to a journey of slavery in a strange land. Nevertheless, he served his master with all his heart and facilitated the expansion of his master's business. This made his master to commit everything he had into his hand. As time went by, someone who was close to his master's rib, the flower of his heart, thought of surrendering the honey of her husband in her possession to the boy, but he rejected it and ran away. He told her that he will never taste of his master's honey. She endeavoured to force him into taking it, praise the lord, he maintained his stand.

The wife of his master who was seriously working towards covering her shame made a wrong accusation about him to his master. And due to the fact that he was ignorant of his truthfulness in service he sent him to prison. Fortunately, this experience led to his promotion and hon. our. The narrative above is about Joseph who was the eleventh child of his father. He was born when Rachel told Jacob "...*Give me children, or else I die*" Jacob cherished him beyond his brothers and this led to him been sold into slavery. Joseph served in truth and brought increase to Potiphar. Surprisingly, Potiphar's wife intended to give her body to Joseph. Though, he rejected she endeavoured to force him. He demonstrated truthfulness in service to God and man, as a result, left his cloth and ran away. This made his master sho was ignorant of his truthful disposition in service to send him to prison. "...*the scripture cannot be broken...*"(John 10:35b) "...*all things work together for good to them that love God, to them who are called according to his purpose*" God turned the prison to a channel of promotion.

2. Serve Him Wholeheartedly: Deut 11: 13-14. "*And it shall come to pass, if ye shall hearken diligently unto my commandments which I command you this day, to love the LORD your God, and to serve him with all your heart and with all your soul, That I will give you the rain of your land in his due season...*" God appreciates wholehearted service. It prompts Him to fulfill His promises in our lives.

The rain represents anything you need for advancement in life. From provision, connection, fortification, libration, divine inspiration to perfection. God is ready to release the rain of His grace and favour that will activate the reality of His will in your life.

Wholehearted service is a two way thing we serve God and carry out service to men. The same way God rewards your service towards Him He rewards your service to humanity. Sometimes your reward comes inform of appreciation and good will. Such was the service of Dr Godwin Maduka, a United State of America based from Umuchukwu in Orumba South Local GovernmentArea of Anambra State formerly known as Nkerefi a place that was hitherto known as one of the background and remote communities in the state. The village was only known for kidnapping, poverty and other criminal acts. Thanks to God the wholehearted service of Dr Godwin Maduka to the community brought a great change. He compelled the Governor of the state to construct two major roads connecting Umuchukwu to neighbouring communities and his organisation was to be responsible for 50% of the cost of the project. He further built,

- Two churches.
- Trinity hospital and maternity.

- Over 100 houses for widows and the poor.
- Immaculate international college 1and 2 with buses donated to them.
- A police station.
- A magistrate court.
- Barracks for the civil defense staff.
- Community and village hall.
- Post office.
- State High Court.
- Provided transformers to boost electricity.
- Mighty edifices for primary and secondary schools.
- Built a palace for the monarch.
- Built for five star hotel known as Lion of Africa.
- !5 storey tall building world class international standard hospital/ research institute.
- Sponsored scholarships.
- Vocational centers and many others. He changed all the thatched houses to four bedroom flats. This wholehearted service has left everyone in awl and lasting celebration. This is because he has done what the State and Federal government were not able to achieve for the village of Nkerefi.

3. Do not replace your service for God with earthly pursuit: Matt 6: 24 *"... ye cannot serve God and mammon."* Mammon here means money and material things. You must be a heavenly minded servant who gives priority to God's call in all things. You must recognize the position and superior authority of God in your decision making, aspirations, marital ambition and conversation. You must have a burning passion to put God first in all things. Your commitment to God is not limited to the attitude of others but, God's expectation over your life

It is not an offense for a minister to be a businessman. Your business must not take your heart and attention away from God. You are to use it as a tool to promote and expand God's kingdom. Therefore, your passion for the word of God, holiness, evangelism, prayer, love and building of God's kingdom should not diminish.

4. Serve Him faithfully: 1 Corinthians 4:2...*it is required in stewards that a man be found faithful."*
A lot of people are afraid to keep church money in their custody. The distance between you and the money is not the problem but, how faithful you are. Faithfulness does not only keep you away from stealing it also enable you to give proper account of anything in your custody. Your faithfulness is not determined by the presence of others. It is determined by your relationship with God.
Faithfulness demands that you obey God's directive in giving, evangelization, life's ambition and as well as in your marriage. God rejected Saul because he was not faithful in the Lord's battle, Gehazi because he went contrary to his master's directive and fifty eight of Christ disciples because they did not follow him till the end.

I learnt if a lady who has been praying for the will of God in marriage for a very long time. Not knowing that God has answered and someone has been led to her.

Unfortunately, the confirmation of the answer requires she identify with those who are not yet married despite the fact that she going to fifty years. But, she failed in this regard. When the general overseer of her church made an announcement that all the singles should stand up, she sat down due to shame and the man that was led to her assumed that he was making a mistake and married someone else. Unfaithfulness in identifying with spinsters which emanated from her age made her to miss the blessing. Do not allow your age to affect your obedience. While you are thinking that time is gone concerning your challenges, remember that God is time. If He says there is still time for Sarah at 89 years never accept fate and fail God's test at the brink of your breakthrough.

Pastor Adeboye also gave a sad testimony about someone who he prayed for and God opened a door of breakthrough for him. In the cause of their discussion he asked the man if he would be faithful in thanking God by paying his tithe: to his surprise the man became furious and replied that, that was his first breakthrough God should wait for another time before talking of tithe, while he wanted to live his office in anger pastor Adeboye apologized that he was sorry for his statement.

What happened was that after the prayer of the man of God someone called him to sell his property at Ikoyi at any amount and bring certain percentage to him. After he sold the property, but refused to honour God with his tithe or respect the man of God by being humble while discussing with him and acting at his directive. When he got to the man to give him the amount he requested, the man denied asking him to sell his property and threatened to arrest him if he goes near that property. He ran back to the man of God and asked him to pray for him again, but, pastor Adeboye said the battle is between him and God therefore, he cannot render any prayer. Unfaithfulness in tithe and honour of God's servant finished him.

5. Serve Him till death: Joshua 24:14-15 *"Now therefore fear the LORD, and serve him in sincerity and in truth: and put away the gods which your fathers served on the other side of the flood, and in Egypt: and serve ye the LORD. And if it seem evil unto you to serve the LORD "choose you this day whom ye will serve; whether the gods which your fathers served that were on the other side of the flood, or the gods of the Amorites, in whose land ye dwell: but as for me and my house we will serve the LORD."* In verse 29 it says *"…Joshua the son of Nun, the servant of the LORD, died, being an hundred and ten years old."* And this was the record of the scripture concerning Joshua in verse 31: *And Israel served the LORD all the days of Joshua…"*

This must be our goal, serving the lord till the end. God does not want us to stop our journey half way. HE desires that we come to him in heaven. It grieves His spirit when saints backslide as a result of the blessings He given them. Though, threats, test, tough circumstances and temptation awaits us on the way, we must be resolute in our pursuit of serving God.

Chapter Seven

THE TEST OF GOD'S WILL

James, the son of Zebedee, was a fisherman by trade when Jesus called him to a lifetime ministry. James' faith in Christ was tested. While defending his faith at the point of tribulation, the Roman officer who guarded him watched in amazement and became convinced. He declared his new faith to the Judge and knelt beside James to accept beheading as a Christian.

Test is paramount to true children of God. It comes in different dimensions to confirm our confession and advance our profession and call into ministry. James, the son of Zebedee's test proved his readiness to obey God's will at any cost and it led to the conversion of the Roman officer. Your test, though challenging, is a process through which God glorifies his son, Jesus and makes you a light to the world. It may come in the form of rejection, demotion, castration, starvation, execution and oppression. Identifying with Jesus amidst difficult situations that are intended to test you guarantees your coronation in glory.

Fortunately, the presence of the Holy Spirit gives us victory over test of life and faith. Your willingness to yield to the voice of the Holy Spirit fortifies your inner man and makes you unstoppable.

Key Areas Where We Are Tested

Some of the major areas of test are,

- Your belief,
- Your stand,
- Your love,
- Your commitment,
- Your patience.

Your belief on 'God's will' will be tested: How firm is your belief in God's word and his programme for your life?

Mordecai's believe was tested. The Jews were only permitted to bow down to God alone. This made Mordecai, Haman's enemy to be angry. Mordecai was in a tight corner because the king commanded everyone to prostrate when greeting him. Therefore, Mordecai's refusal to prostrate was direct to the king and not Haman. But he held his belief in God's commandment in high esteem than anyone.

Esther 3: 5-6 "…*when Haman saw that Mordecai bowed not, nor did him reverence, then was Haman full of wrath. And he thought scorn to lay hands on Mordecai; for they had shown him the people of Mordecai: wherefore Haman sought to destroy all the Jews that were throughout the kingdom of Ahasuerus, even the people of Mordecai.*"

Let us focus on ourselves a little. You are to have a firm resolve and backbone that strengthens your inner man to face any test. You need to ascertain whether you have made any resolve by answering the following questions.

Do you believe that you do not need to mess up with any man or woman or dress indecently to secure a job or find a life partner? Your belief will be tested.
Your body is the temple of the Holy Ghost therefore, it is held in high esteem by the Trinity. Anyone who defiles his or her body for any reason will not experience the fullness of God's purpose for their lives.

A sister found herself in an organization that mandated women to dress indecently and she obliged because of money. But, due to the fact that her husband was a pastor in a bible believing church, she was told to drop the job. It was indeed a difficult situation because jobs are not easy to come by. As she made up her mind and obeyed, God opened a great door that connected her to highly placed people in the society and she began to make money with less stress. Your decision to stand out from the crowd attracts supernatural connection into heaven's treasure and blessings for your life.

Do you believe that abortion is the same as murder? Your belief will be tested.
A sister got pregnant during her maternity leave. She already has three kids. During the third month of her maternity leave, she conceived. Since her boss has threatened that if she gets pregnant any more she would be laid off. She hated the experience and planned a way out of her pregnancy or if possible, make it unknown to her boss. But unfortunately for her, immediately, she got into the office and was discussing with her boss,

nature betrayed her and she excused herself to use the toilet. Her boss did not give her time before reacting and mandating her to terminate the pregnancy. In her state of confusion, she discussed the issue with her colleague who also gave her the same counsel. While she was thinking of what to do, she remembered that abortion is murder and she does not want to kill an innocent child and become a murderer. More so, she remembered that she waited for two years after her wedding before she conceived. The fact that she does not want to be a murderer and that she must not sin against God who delivered her from the reproach of barrenness, she declined from aborting the pregnancy. Therefore, she was relieved of her job. She took the situation in good faith. Fortunately, after a while, her husband was transferred abroad. This necessitated the relocation of every member of the family. She gave birth abroad after which she had another child overseas. Your destiny is in the hands of God.

Do you believe that you are to remain with your spouse till death whatever the situation?
Circumstances will arise in your marriage that will test your belief when it seems as if there is delay either in finance or child bearing or when there are challenges in the family. Be ready, God wants you to triumph.

Do you believe that seeking God with all your heart is capable of prospering you?
Your belief will be tested. A brother lost his job because he was told to carry a carton of alcohol and he refused. God

proved Himself faithful and gave him a better job. He lost his job as a driver but he got another job where he was made the supervisor of drivers in a petroleum company. You cannot escape the test of your belief, and the word of God cannot be broken. It is written"... *Till heaven and earth shall pass, one jot or one tittle shall in no wise pass from the law, till all be fulfilled.*" This means that no matter the test, what God has planned for you will definitely come to pass in Jesus name. You must be ready to see the end of the testimony.

Now we need to come back to our discussion in the book of Esther. Every Christian must be resolute like Mordecai. We must not allow people who do not have the fear of God to bend our conviction of holiness unto the Lord. As the devil and his agents have been persistent in getting true Christians, Haman too persisted on his mission against Mordecai. In Esther 3:8 "...*Haman said unto the king Ahasuerus, There is a certain people in all the provinces of thy kingdom: and their laws are diverse from all people; neither keep they the king's law: therefore it is not for the king's profit to suffer them. If it please the king, let it be written that they may be destroyed: and I will pay ten thousand talents of silver to the hands of those that have the charge of the business, to bring it into the king's treasuries.*" Mordecai never thought that his belief will take him this far. It has gotten to the point where circumstances facing him are intending to bend his conviction by force.

You may come across difficult situations in life that sin seems inevitable. At such moments if you get involved in self-pity you will fall: but, if you see yourself as fighting the battle of the Lord. You will be strengthened from on high.

Thank God Nehemiah persisted despite the fact that the test has gotten to its peak.

Your test may take a different dimension. You may be faced with peer or family pressure that wants you to feel ashamed for your belief. A girl who is privileged to be a virgin in today's world may be ridiculed by her friends to the point that she sees it as a taboo to be chaste.

You must learn from Mordecai and avoid giving in to any challenge that the enemy brings your way. To overcome the test against your belief you must;

1. Pray,
2. Press on.
3. Put your trust in Jesus,
4. Pull down discouragement,
5. Ponder on God's word,
6. Partner with champions in the faith,
7. Persevere.

Your stand on 'God's will' would be tested: Your stand matters: the stand of the angels cast down Satan from heaven. The stand of Moses made Pharaoh to release the Israelites. The stand of Meshach, Shadrach and Abednego revealed the presence and supremacy of Christ to the Babylonians and the stand of Rechabites condemned the rebellion of Israel. It can move mountains, change history, reverse hopeless situations, subdue the works of darkness and bring you into the actualization of your destiny.

Your stand on God's will and your faith work together while fear and fall go together. Jacob stood on his request of blessing from the angel despite the fact that his thigh was out of joint, until his name was changed to Israel. God celebrates those who stand on his will for their lives. Jacob was called a prince who "had power with God and man" because he stood on God's will for his life.

Whenever your stand on God's will is challenged, God is about to make a hero out of your life. Please, during the time of your test, do not look at how many times you have fasted and how long you have been praying. Look *"unto Jesus the author and finisher of our faith"*. The secret of our victory is faith and obedience on God's word.

Your love for 'God's will' would be tested: *"AND it came to pass after these things, that God did tempt Abraham, and said unto him, Abraham: and he said, Behold, here I am. And He said, Take now thy son, thine only son Isaac, whom thou lovest, and get thee into the land of Moriah; and offer him there for a burnt offering..."*
Abraham's love for God was tested. God did not request for what will cost him nothing, rather he requested for the crown of his joy and existence. Majority today will rather behave as if they did not receive any directive. Whenever God leads them towards a breakthrough, they recognize his voice and act promptly and they return with a testimony. But whenever God's leading is contrary to their expectation they behave as if it is the voice of a demon and neglect such directives. For instance, if God leads them to give a brother or sister a huge sum of money, they begin to question such directives from the

spirit of God and make effort to silence it. Others will resist any voice that leads them from a well paid job into a full time ministry.

While ministers who love comfort rather than God's will concerning the salvation of souls will never move an inch whenever they are inspired to leave their comfort zone where they are being nourished with the treasury of God's children to a place of sacrificial service for God.

How to pass the test of your love for God's will
The fact that God reveals Himself to you in a greater dimension whenever He discovers that your love has increased for his will makes it important for you to pass the test of your love for God's will.
The following prepares the ground for you to pass God's test.

1. **Be dead to self**: Self is the chief enemy of man. The moment self is dead in your life, you become inaccessible to defeat. It makes you alive in the spirit of the resurrected Christ. Your life reflects the word of God and puts failure during your moment of test at a distance. Jesus fought self at Gethsemane in order to pass the test of His love for God's will. His victory over self after three hours of prayer produced the strength to face the cross.

2. Move at God's pace: Contentment and patience helped Jeremiah to move at the pace of God's leading for his life. His love for God's will was tested when God told him that if he does not rise up and speak to the Israelites, he would be confounded before them. Jeremiah's task was a difficult one because the Israelites in his days were adamant to the word of God. Continuing in such a task confirmed his love for God's will.

If you fail to go at the pace of God's leading, your love for God's will is questionable. It seemly means that the love of what makes patience impossible in your life is more than your love for God's will. It may be a woman, money, popularity, promotion or taking vengeance. If you discover that you are finding it difficult to go at God's pace, pray because you may end up in hell or miss out from God's purpose for your life.

Circumstances at the moment may not encourage you to go at God's pace, but you need to be determined and be obedient in all things. Despite the fact that David found himself in an unpleasant and insecure situation, he ensured that he moved at the pace of God. If he had decided to kill Saul, he would be operating at his own pace to achieve God's will for his life as the successor of Saul. He refrained himself from killing him because the will of God that stood as a shield for Saul was *"Touch not my anointed and do my prophet no harm"* He passed the test of his love for God's will and in the end, he still fulfilled God's plan for his life.

3. Do not respond to your emotions: Most actions that are inspired by mere emotion rather than knowledge do not enable us to reach the peak of God's will for our lives. Saul, Demas, Samson, the Israelites in the wilderness and so on missed God's best because their actions during the moments of their trials originated from emotion and not the knowledge of God's will. Any feeling that you refuse to subject in the light of God's word would cost more than you can pay. If a person who is supposed to be a man of God deliberately reproaches you as a result of challenges of life, you may not feel like forgiving or praying for him. But God expects that you forgive those who trespass against you. Therefore, you are to bury every pain that his offense has caused and forgive him from your heart.

A man that was laid off from his job because his colleague was aiming at his position. The colleague successfully planted hatred in the mind of his boss toward him by laying false allegation against him. The boss had no choice than to send him away. When he was laid off, God opened a better door for him that made him earn money in dollars. In the course of time, the man who influenced his dismissal from his formal organization called to apologise and request for financial support from him. He had no choice but to forgive and at the same time, send him some amount of money. You cannot do such if you give priority to feelings and not to the word of God.

We are to leave our battles for Jesus and He will give us the victory in Jesus' name. Amen.

4. Cast your cares upon him: Cares of life gives us concern and if you fail to approach what is giving you concern with faith, you may be negatively influenced and fail the test of God's will for your life. Focusing on your losses rather than the possibility in God's faithfulness and power weakens your consecration and dependence on God.

God holds the key to our cares. Therefore we must not allow them to affect our relationship with Him. John Bunyan cast his care on God and God glorified Himself in his life. His imprisonment that was intended to stop him became a source of inspiration that helped him to write his popular book that has been translated into 200 languages. Imagine such an opportunity! Your trials should not quench the love of God in your life. The fact that your test can unfold greater revelation, manifestation of God's power and divine connection should guide our decisions and actions whenever our love for God is tested.

Your commitment would be tested: Your readiness to do God's will opens new doors of opportunities and responsibilities which attract new challenges. Challenges like building a new church when there is financial constraints, raising an invincible work force when only few people are willing to consecrate, being transferred to a new environment for ministerial purposes and facing personal and family problems all stands to test our commitment.

Whatever the challenge, our attitude should be like that of Zachariah and Elizabeth, Paul and Silas, and others who continued in their commitment despite the test they faced. John the Baptist was a product of God's blessing and faithfulness for a committed family.

The money and time spent as a chorister may stand as test, the smell in church toilet as test to a cleaner, the rigor in book writing and financial involvement as test to an author, confrontation of the power of darkness against one's health and family as test to the prayer warrior, the presence of multiple needs as test to a giver and the presence of false brethren as test to one who is hospitable.

God's reason for testing your commitment is to take you higher and attest to your love and desire to serve Him. It may not be easy at the moment but be rest assured that God by His love and mercy will turn things around for you.

Your commitment in praying for others, singing ministry, giving, evangelism, follow up and counseling, cleaning the church, hospitality and every good work you do will be rewarded.

The Back Bone that Overcomes our Test of Commitment
"The righteous also shall hold on his way, and he that hath clean hands shall be stronger and stronger." (Job 17:9)
The righteous would hold on his way of commitment when there is faith, patience and prayer.

How faith backs up commitment
The period of test is when people ask a lot of questions that kill their pursuit of commitment to God. That is why we need faith to maintain our commitment to God.

The foundation of faith that keeps us committed.

    a.   Faith in God,

b.   Faith in God's word,

c.   Faith in God's will,

d.   Faith in God's works.

(a) Faith in God: God is the first and the last. He is
Jehovah Nissi – Lord our Man of War,
Jehovah Shammah – The Lord is Nigh,
Jehovah Rohi – The Lord our Shepherd,
Jehovah El- Shadia – The all sufficient God,
Jehovah Jireh – The Great Provider,
Jehovah Rapha – The Lord Our Healer,
Jehovah Shalom – The Lord our Peace.

We all have the knowledge of God's greatness but during our moments of test Satan uses discouragement to make us doubt God's faithfulness and ability to turn our challenges to triumph. This results into lukewarmness. Take Joseph for instance, though he was committed to his father and to God, this did not stop him from experiencing slavery and imprisonment. However, his faith in God did not diminish. He told his brethren in Genesis 45:7-8 "...*God sent me before you to preserve you a posterity in the earth, and to save your lives by a great deliverance. So now it was not you that sent me hither, but God...*" Without strong faith in God for who He is that He will never fail no matter the surrounding circumstances, he could not have held on to the dream that God revealed to him when he was young.

(b) Faith in God's Word: God's word is basic to our existence. Rather than abandoning your commitment to God, you are supposed to hold on to God's word. This is because He said: *"heaven and earth shall pass away: but my words shall not pass away."* God also said in Isaiah 55:11 *"So shall my word be that goeth forth out of my mouth: It shall not return unto me void, but it shall accomplish that which I please, and it shall prosper in the thing whereto I sent it. For ye shall go out with joy and be led forth with peace: the mountains... shall break forth before you into singing, and all the trees of the fields shall clap their hand".*

When you combine the words of God and that of Jesus it should spark up a solid faith in your heart that keeps you committed in whatever circumstance. God created the world without any resources but through the instrumentality of the word. Therefore, your trust on His word carries a potential solution that will turn all things to work for your good. And in Psalm 125:1 says that *"They that trust in the LORD shall be as mount Zion, which cannot be removed, but abideth forever."* God wants you to take encouragement from His word. It provides light amidst darkness, possibility amidst impossibility, hope amidst hopelessness and wonders beyond comprehension. It makes your commitment immoveable in moments of test.

(c) Faith in God's Will: The reward of God's will for our lives should be the motivating factor that makes us to persist in commitment. We must have a strong resolve that will empower us to keep to God's will. God's will in the life of Abraham, Elijah, Peter and Daniel were fulfilled, it will be fulfilled in your life. I learnt of a sister who had revelation that she will conceive and the revelation did not come to fulfillment the year she had it. It took some years before it came to reality. When it seems as if you do not know what to do; you have fasted, others have fasted on your behalf and anointed men of God had prayed for you, do not turn back from wholehearted service and fellowship with God. He will soon bring you out of any situation that stands as a test to your commitment and His will for you will be fulfilled in Jesus' name.

(d) Faith in God's Works: God wants you to take a clue from His works in the lives of committed Christian who experienced moments of intense test but came out triumphantly. Pastor W, F Kumuyi, Pastor E.A Adeboye, John Bunyan, Billy Graham and a host of other soldiers in Christ are all examples of how God deals with His children who persist in their commitment towards His call for their lives. God never changes His standard of faithfulness. Abraham was faithful and committed in obeying God's command for him to sacrifice his son, and his seed became a blessing to the world. Solomon also showed faithfulness in his commitment; he sacrificed a thousand Rams and God made him the richest and wisest on earth. He preserved Meshach, Shadrach and Abednego who were committed to defending the faith in the fire and Daniel who was committed in interceding for Israel in the lion's den. He anointed the apostles who were committed in their consecration in Israel and Babalola that was committed to soul winning in Africa. God is still the same today. Whatever the challenge is confronting your commitment today, it will give way, because, God who worked in the lives of those who were committed to Him in times past is working in your life.

The Place of Patience in Commitment.
Patience enables the continuity of commitment despite testing circumstances. Patience must have her perfect work in our lives to facilitate our triumph. Patience requires you let God and let go.

It makes you dead to self and be alive to God's will. You do not compare yourself with others in a carnal manner rather, you consistently look unto Jesus, the author and finisher of our faith.

- Are you worshipping in a place where no one makes friends with you due to your financial status?
- Have you been deprived of promotion because your commitment to God's work does not allow you to stay long at work?
- Are you lacking anything that makes even so called believers to make jest of you?
- Are you faced with a long term battle with the powers of darkness because of your calling?

- Is your boss or lecturer trying to confront and frustrate your life? Do not take any carnal decision. Be certain that God is conscious of everything you are going through. He will definitely turn your test to testimony in Jesus' name. Amen.

Your patience will be tested.
The greater part of Christians are failing God's test in this

area. You must be ready to make up your mind in this area because the majority of Christians will miss the rapture as a result of certain character of impatience they exhibit flagrantly You cannot be a success as a Christian without patience. It reveals the level of our maturity in Christ Jesus.

How does God test our Patience?
1.God test our patience when he deliberately delays our deliverance from persecution: Hajia Binta Faruk was born in Muri Kingdom and got married to the younger brother of Shewu of Bornu in 1999 she encountered a believer called Chinwe in University of Nsukka. She testified that Chinwe loved to sing praises. Therefore, she sought for ways to deal with her. One day, when Chinwe came back from the fellowship, she kept her Bible on Binta's bed. When she saw it, she requested for who kept it on her bed. Chinwe apologized but before she finished, Binta tore her Bible and dealt with her. Chinwe took the pieces of the Bible and cried to heaven, then, called her name thrice and told Binta that she would preach the gospel with the Bible she tore. And that pronouncement came to pass after seven years. Binta had always been happy seeing Christians persecuted but on the 25th of September, 1999 the story changed. Binta saw an unusual bright light around 1:30a.m on Saturday. The light came with a bright wind which blew and threw the pictures on the wall and other valuables on the ground. She and her husband became afraid. Her husband got up from the bed and brought out charms. He placed it on the ground with a charcoal but the wind threw it away.

Thereafter, she heard a thunderous voice which says "You have been baptized in the Holy Spirit. Go and be "Tabitha" unto my people". She asked her husband if he could understand what the voice is saying but he said he did not hear any voice. He assumed that his wife was a cultist that is why she was hearing a voice he did not hear. He concluded that she was trying to sacrifice him or their set of twins. He took their twins to the quest room and abandoned her in the bedroom. Binta was unable to sleep. She said she heard the voice again in the morning asking her to tell her husband that she has received Jesus as her personal Lord and Saviour. She refused, insisting that a Fulani girl has nothing to do with Jesus.

Binta thought that she had a demon, but the message was repeated on 28th and 29th. Each time, she was told to come and serve the body of Christ. She told her husband that she would be going to Church on Saturday. He reacted immediately, and said that it would never happen in his house. Though it came as a surprise to him, Binta started to feel the joy of Salvation and decided to do God's will. She bought a Bible that Saturday hid it in her box and took it to a church on Sunday. That was how her persecution started. Her children, car and other belongings were taken. She was sacked from NTA Jalingo and chained by her family for seven days. She was later released with death threat if she attended Church again. While her mother made effort to settle the dispute between her and her father through the help of her uncle, her father shut at her but God did not allow the bullet to penetrate.

The little adjustment she made helped saved her from the

gunshot. Later, she was told to live with another of her uncle. He threatened to kill her with cutlass. Her father went further to imprison her. And she was there for six months. As God would have it, some people on prison evangelism heard that she was imprisoned because of her faith. So, they notified the chairman of CAN (Christian Association of Nigeria) who wrote a petition that led to proper trial. She was sentenced to two years imprisonment and Five thousand Naira fine which was settled by one of the Christian Women Fellowship in the area. She was imprisoned from 5th September, 2000 and after she prayed, she was miraculously released on 8th October, 2000.

Two months later, after her release, she decided to go and reach out to her grandparents. On getting there, the youths in the village were already looking for her. Therefore, they made efforts to hide her but when their efforts failed, she ran to the bush. She spent four days in the bush. On the fourth day, she saw a snake close to where she was. This and all her experiences made her to tell the Lord that she cannot continue again. Christ told her that the snake would have beaten her if He had not shut its mouth. Binta was told that she cannot backslide at this point with the level of persecution she had suffered. So, she repented from her intention to return to Egypt(sin).

Before her release from prison, God had used her to minister to a Christian whose womb was shut because she married a man from another religion. Binta told her that the barrenness was as a result of her action. The barren woman was prayed for by Binta and by the grace of God, a few months after the prayer, the woman conceived. This conception made both the woman and her husband to turn to the Lord in genuine repentance. Binta's persecution however continued intensely. No one would be able to continue in faith with such persecutions without patience. At another occasion, Moslem youths kidnapped her and raised their cutlasses to kill her but their hands hung in the air. It happened to three of them, so, others fled. They were arrested by the police who intended to kill them. When she was invited to the police station, she prayed for them and their hands and cutlasses came down. She also pleaded for their release. Those youth gave their lives to Christ.

At every occasion that she was kidnapped, God frustrated the counsel of the enemy. When Binta saw the hand of God upon her, she made a resolution to start preaching to the Fulani people. She also made up her mind to go to the Middle East and establish a church in Saudi Arabia. It takes patience to sustain your conviction amidst persecution while you are expecting God to put an immediate end to such persecution. Despite the persecution from the enemy she is now being used by God to take care of all who were persecuted for their faith. She has 49 of such persecuted Christians under her roof. This is aside many of the fact that many of her family members have given their lives to Jesus. Her husband continued his persecution despite the fact that he saw a lot of converts. While he was chasing her with assassins, he got accident and lost his life. Binta has established Tabitha Evangelistic Ministry, Jalingo, Jos, Plateau State, Nigeria. It is not easy when your persecutions seem perpetual but as you continue in your commitment of being faithful to God, He will turn things around and your desires will be granted.

2. When your spouse seems not to meet up with your expectations in terms of his or her character or support towards your purpose in life. A man who was a drunkard respected his wife because she had never said anything negative or allowed his drunkenness to interfere with her submission and love for him. One day, while he was drinking with his friends they began to make jest of Christians. They said, nowadays Christians are not real. The man immediately told them that he knows one Christian that is real. In amazement they ask who that Christian could be. He told them that it was his wife. They laugh him to scorn, claiming that it is because she had not been tested. So, he permitted them to come and test her. It was not a pleasant situation, but the patience of the woman made it a glorious opportunity to reveal the grace of God.

3. When God's will contradicts your feelings: This was the experience of David when he requested from God if he should pursue the enemy but God said that he should wait until he sees some signs on the tree.

4. When God's timing for you to take certain decisions in your life is later than you expect: Moses launched out for his purpose at age 40 but God called him when he was 80 years. His impatience added 30 years to Israel's captivity in Egypt. Though the people of Israel were being oppressed, God still expected Moses to wait for an additional 10 years. God told Abraham that his descendants will spend 400 years in Egypt, but spent 430 years. This was as a result of the impatience.

5. When you are reproached, rebuked or misrepresented for no reason: Jeremiah had similar experience but, in the end, God favoured him.

6. When you are faced with a great challenge that makes you feel that compromise is the best option: - Job's intense persecution aimed at moving him from his relationship with God, as that of his wife was moved. Yet, patience gave him more than he has lost during the persecution.

It is through difficult situations that your faith is made stronger and your spiritual worth is proved.

OUTSTANDING QUALITIES THAT STABILIZES OUR PATIENCE

1. Endurance,
2. Temperance,
3. Perseverance,
4. Tolerance,
5. Reliance,
6. Abstinence (fasting)
7. Observance,

1. Endurance: *"Blessed is the man that endureth temptation: for when he is tried, he shall receive the crown of life..."* (James 1:12) Endurance empowered Jacob to marry to his dream wife, Rachel and advanced till he became two bands. It stood as the foundation upon which he pushed and built his destiny. The possibility he experienced on that great morning when he entered a new platform of glory and greatness and his name was changed to Israel is a product of endurance. Many people have at one occasion or the other missed God's blessing for their lives due to lack of this all important virtue.

2. Temperance: The anchor of Paul's ministry was temperance. The devil did everything to stop him knowing the magnitude of his impact on the world. Yet, he ended as a conqueror. Things like discouragement, lack, neglect of the brethren, pain and lengthiness of his persecution would have shown him the way out if he failed to control himself. He made this known when he said "...*I keep under my body, and bring it into subjection...*" (1cor 9:27a) Test has a way of softly reducing your passion and concentration. It is aimed at making you half hearted in your pursuit to do God's will. But temperance gives you the ability to press forward and maintain a steady ride in faith. The string of endurance will cut if temperance is missing.

3. Perseverance: Wilson Churchill, Thomas Edison and many others perseveringly charted their way into fulfillment despite the setbacks they had.

4. Tolerance: Tolerance enables us to overcome the devil's arrow of provocation. The more you tolerate people, the less you are provoked. It does not mean that you should act like Eli who could not rebuke evil in the life of his children. It simply means that we do not allow the sin of others to affect our relationship with God like Moses. Moses was the meekest in the earth and has been tolerating the excesses of children of Israel but a time came when he decided to make them aware of the gravity of their offences. Therefore, he called them rebels and smote the rock rather than speaking into it as commanded. God did not spare him. He missed the promised land! Consistent tolerance enables us to exercise patience whatever betides.

5. Reliance: God is the basis of the patience of Abraham, Ruth, Elisha and David. Except you consistently look unto Jesus you will faint. Relying on God is a powerful tool. It shines light into your life. Your life becomes unpredictable to the enemy. When you find yourself in the fire of the enemy, you will not be burnt. The lion's den of the wicked will become a place of relaxation. God does the miraculous when we rely on him. Finally, it brings into the company of those *"who through faith subdued kingdoms, wrought righteousness, obtained promises, stopped the mouths of lions, quench the violence of fire, escaped the edge of the sword, out of weakness were made strong, waxed valiant in fight, turned to flight the armies of the alien, women received their dead raised to life again: and others were tortured, not accepting deliverance; that they might obtain a better resurrection."* (Heb 11:33-35)

6. Abstinence: Patience is a virtue that must take hold of the totality of your life if continuity in 'God's will' will be assured. Such patience requires grace. Abstinence here is referring to fasting and prayer. Fasting subdues the flesh and strengthens your inner man. You receive sufficient grace to face and prevail in any situation.

People who do not set any time apart to wait on the Lord are spiritually weak. They are being controlled by their flesh in most cases. They always find it difficult to walk in the spirit which works out patience in us. Your moment of waiting on the Lord is a time of supernatural renewal. God sends His word and divine revelation which will build and prepare your heart for tough moments. You must create time to wait on the Lord. It has been proven to be the tool of express growth in patience and spiritual maturity.

7. Observance: Holy Ghost led observation is a key to our pursuit of patience in life and ministry. Observation helps us to meditate on God's will and discern the trick of the enemy over our lives. There are occasions when God expects patience from us in other to access His best for our lives. In most cases, Satan introduces alternatives that look like divine intervention except we prayerfully make a critical observation of our thoughts and ambition, we may fall out of God's plan for our lives.

Christ exemplified the principle of observation when He rejected the counsel of those who intended to make Him king. God's will for Him was that He would be a Prophet, Priest and in the end, King in that order. He was already a Prophet as at when they wanted to make Him a King but He has not fulfilled His purpose of being the Priest. As Prophet, He has spoken the word and the mind of God to humanity. This is found in Deut 18:18 God said *"I will raise them up a Prophet from among their brethren, like unto thee, and will put my words in his mouth; and he shall speak unto them all that I shall command him.*" And it was confirmed in John 17:8 "*...I have given unto them the words which thou gavest me...*" He was yet to fulfill His purpose as a Priest. The Priest is to take the blood of the lamb into the holy of holies to intercede for the sin of the people.

Those who came to make him king were ignorant of God's purpose for His life. Since He knew His purpose as God expects you to know yours, He rejected their offer of making Him King. But haven fulfilled His purpose of being a priest on the cross by sacrificing himself for our sins as He said in Matthew 26:28 that "*...this is my blood... which is shed for... the remission of sin.*" And it was fulfilled in Matthew 27:50 "*Jesus, when he had cried again with a loud voice, yielded up the ghost. And, behold the veil of the temple was rent in twain from the top to the bottom...*" This is the veil that shielded everyone from the holy of holies as the High priest goes in once a year with the blood of the lamb to atone for the sins of the people. The power of Christ's crucifixion rent (tore) it into two. This confirms that the yearly sacrifice done by the High priest is no longer needed.

Christ has sacrificed His blood once for the salvation of humanity. He is automatically occupying His status as the King of Kings. Though, this will physically materialize at the millennial reign. Moreover, He is not coming to reign as a King over sinners. His Kingdom is for saints who will make it at the rapture and those that will later join them in heaven by paying for their salvation with their blood at the great tribulation. That is why the scripture enjoins that all things should be done decently

Dakarabor David

and in order.

Chapter Eight

THE POWER OF GOD'S WILL

Unspeakable possibilities await those who discipline themselves and determined to follow through on God's will in every area of their lives. God's will is final. Anytime God is set to accomplish His will, no power on earth, in heaven, in the sea or under the earth can alter His intention. It can only be altered if we refuse to play our part which is prompt obedience, total reliance on God and perseverance.

God can do anything to establish His will. Let us consider a few of what God does to perfect His will. It can be found in the word POWER. God can:

P – Prove His supremacy and pull down barriers.

O - Organise events and order our steps.

W – Work wonders and awake our consciousness.

E – Enclose facts and eliminate our enemies.

R – Reverse evil conclusions and raise us up.

Let us comprehensively consider the points above. Whenever God is to fulfill His will, He always:

P – Prove His supremacy: God proves Himself supreme in the contest between the power of light and of darkness that determines event on earth. It is not surprising that Satan and his agents always endeavour to set up their own will on earth. Yet, God remains who He is. His *"… dominion is an everlasting dominion, and his kingdom is from generation to generation. And all the inhabitants of the earth are reputed as nothing: and he doeth according to his will in the army of heaven, and none can stay his hand, or say unto him, What doest thou?"* (Daniel 4:34a-35)

Realities of life and events in the Bible have revealed how God proves Himself supreme in the world. The house of Voltaire the French writer who said the Bible will be out of existence in 100years was later purchased and used to print and circulate the Bible. I learnt of an herbalist who aimed at hindering God's will for man's salvation in Lagos. He did everything to resist the success of a crusade that was to be held in his environment. Yet, God proved Himself supreme. The herbalist died a day to the crusade and the crusade was held successfully; to God's glory, a lot of people gave their lives to Christ.

More so, Donald Trump made an extraordinary feat when he made Jerusalem Israel's capital city. Though, this has stirred reactions from various countries in the world. It is a confirmation of God's word in 2 Chronicles 6:6 *"… I have chosen Jerusalem, that my name might be there…"* and it agrees with 1Kings 14:21b *"…Jerusalem, the city which the LORD did choose out of all the tribes of Israel, to put his name there…"*This made Zachariah to prophesy in Zachariah 2:10-13 *"Sing and rejoice, O daughter of Zion: for, lo, I come, and I will dwell in the midst of thee, saith the LORD.*

And many nations shall be joined to the LORD in that day, and shall be my people...And the LORD shall inherit Judah his portion in the holy land, and shall choose Jerusalem...Be silent, O all flesh, before the LORD: for he is raised up out of his holy habitation."

The life and ministry of late Bishop Benson Idahosa attested to God's supremacy. When Bishop Benson Idahosa was to commence his ministry, he went to the rulers in Benin to request for a landed property. They gave him a place called evil forest for free. They thought the demons in the forest would harm him. Amazingly, he started to make use of the place and nothing happened to him. God will forever be God! He has what it takes to bring His will to reality.

Events in the Bible also speaks volumes. The finger of His supremacy is clearly revealed beginning from the creation of the world to the destruction of the generation of Noah to the call of Abraham and so on. All these assure us that He reveals Himself supreme. More so, the dramatic overthrow of world powers from the Babylonian empire to the Roman empire that was divided into four and the coming reign of Christ over all tongues and languages are indisputable occurrences that silence any form of doubt as to God's supreme power when pursuing His will.

I decree into your life and ministry that God will prove Himself supreme in your life and family and bring His will to pass in Jesus name, amen.

P – Pulls down barriers: - God wants us to have a strong back bone as regards the pursuit of His will for our lives.

He is dissatisfied whenever His children allow Satan or setback to stop His will for their lives. You must be possessed with the spirit of possibility, do not abandon His will for your life because of fear of the unknown. Allow God to tackle the unknown while you follow His leading and wait for His time.

God pulled down the barrier of the wall of Jericho that stood as a hindrance to His will for the descendants of Abraham. He eliminated Herod who sought the life of the child Jesus as he stood as a barrier against His purpose for His life. Also, when Esau's cruelty stood as a barrier to the directive that God gave Jacob: (to return to his father's house), God silenced that cruelty in Esau and ensured the fulfillment of His purpose for Jacob's life.

Is anything trying to stand as a barrier to the fulfillment of God's will for your life? Let faith come alive in you. Stand on the ground that God is ready to demonstrate His power and work out His will for your life. He will arise and remove any barrier and take you into your promised land.

I learnt of an Alhajah who swore that her daughter will not give birth while she is alive. She has been tormenting the marriage of her daughter. So, they moved to an apartment that was reserved for Christians with challenges. The daughter became pregnant and the pregnancy lasted for more than a year. When the torment got to the peak and it was as if the lady would lost her life during the pregnancy, she told God to have His way. At the moment that she invited God to take over and do as He pleases, the Alhajah died after which she was able to give birth. Your freedom is on the way. You will celebrate over every situation standing as a barrier to God's will for you because He will pull them down in Jesus name, amen.

O – Organize event: God's will never knows impossibility. When He willed that Joseph would be a governor, though it seemed unimaginable and unbelievable, God organized events to suit His plan for Joseph.

In Jeremiah 25:1-12 God sent Jeremiah to prophesy the desolation of Israel which will lead to seventy years captivity in Babylon. In Daniel 9:2 He inspired Daniel during his moments of the study of the word of God that the children of Israel had accomplished the seventy years they were to be in captivity and this propelled Daniel to seek the face of God. What happened "...*in the first year of Cyrus king of Persia, that the word of the LORD by the mouth of Jeremiah might be fulfilled, the LORD stirred up the spirit of Cyrus king of Persia, that he made a proclamation throughout all his kingdom, and put it also in writing, saying, Thus saith Cyrus king of Persia, The LORD God of heaven hath given me all the kingdoms of the earth; and he hath charged me to build him an house at Jerusalem, which is in Judah. Who is there among you of all his people? his God be with him, and let him go up to Jerusalem, which is in Judah, and build the house of the LORD God of Israel...*" (Ezra 1:1-3) God continued His operation and Ezra was used to lead them back to Jerusalem and to build the temple. He also brought Hanani in contact with Nehemiah who asked after the welfare of those in Jerusalem. The answer he got set him praying until the door opened for him to advance God's will. God granted him favour before the king who provided all he needed to build the walls of Jerusalem and he restored justice, judgement and orderliness in Jerusalem.

Have you discovered any promise in the word of God? Or is there anything you are expecting Him to do for you? Do not be discouraged; continue in prayer at the right time; God will organise events to suit His will for your life.

O – Order our steps: God's will follows a divine leading. *"…thine ears shall hear a word behind thee, saying, This is the way, walk ye in it"* (Is 30:21)

The moment God observes that one is prepared to know and to do His will, He commences a process of divine guidance that will facilitate His will in such an individual. God leads through the following ways:

- Dreams
- Counsels
- Impression
- Prophesy
- The Bible
- Anointed books

God determines the method He uses; individual varies. In 2kings 7:1, Elisha declared abundance when there was extreme famine in Israel. Like the man on the right hand of the king, many people would probe such prophecy as a result of doubt, fear and unbelief but God divinely guided the lepers to the source of the provision that confirmed the fulfillment of Elijah's prophecy.

It is unwise to depend only on human effort in the fulfillment of God's will for one's life. You do not need to lobby or bribe anyone to access any blessing that God has given you. All you need is consistent faith and patience.

W- Works Wonders: In June 2015, Barcelona won the champions' league and Neymar put on his famous 100% Jesus bandana. It caused a stir in the world. In 2016 during the Rio Olympics, he repeated the same feat wearing the 100% Jesus bandana as he stood on the podium to collect the football Gold medal. The International Olympics Committee wrote an official protest for his use of the 100% Jesus bandana on the stage that prohibits all religious, commercial or political messages. It was amazing that in August 2017, PSG signed Neymar for a world record fee (yet he is not the best player in the world). His colleagues claimed that the money was beyond calculation.

Neymar distinguished himself amidst the multitude of footballers in the world and defended the faith. While people like him deny knowing Jesus whenever they are privileged to occupy an international position, he identified and speechlessly made Jesus known to the world. God demonstrated His power of wonders by granting him a reward that is beyond man's expectation. People are confused about the amount that awarded and why it was given to him. No one should disturb themselves because he position himself to do God's will of making Christ known to a perishing world and God raised him beyond comprehension. This is to serve as an inspiration to those who knew when he was faced with confrontation from all over the world for putting on 100% Jesus bandana. And the amount he was given is a confirmation that God does wonders whenever He is set to accomplish His of making us the head and not the tail.

Pastor E. A Adeboye shared a testimony of how God perfected His will in His life when he was in danger. In Psalm 91 we are promised long life. But, Pastor Adeboye had an encounter that wanted to contradict God's will of long life for him. He said, they went on a missionary journey and on their way to Ilorin they were to go through a bridge that is between Ilorin and Osogbo that can only contain one car at a time. To their surprise after they climbed the bridge on a high speed, a trailer also came into the bridge facing their car with a very high speed. Pastor Adeboye said he thought everything would end on that bridge because the driver of the trailer did not apply break. But to his surprise, his car and the trailer passed simultaneously. His driver who was extremely afraid asked what happen and Pastor Adeboye told him that God expanded the bridge. The driver kept on echoing the word wonderful until they got to their destination. God specializes in doing wonders whenever He is set to fulfill His will. The creation of the world, the conception of Jesus, His resurrection, ascension and other innumerable things that God has done in our personal lives and in the world reveal His wonder.

God wants you to resist every lie of the devil that always aim at weakening your faith whenever we press towards God's will. A wonder is something you cannot fathom in your limited knowledge. It springs out in a systematic and fascinating manner. Sometimes, beneficiaries of such a pursuit and accomplishment may be rear.

The ministry of Binta, the founder of Tabitha Evangelistic Ministry in Nigeria enjoyed similar possibilities. Her life was preserved from every attempt of her persecutors until they surrendered and started to give their lives to Christ; do not dread any height in life. If it is God's will for your life, He will work it out.

W – Wake Our Consciousness (God's will awakes our consciousness)

Jeremiah was formed from his mother's womb to a prophet whose prophecy would determine events in the world. No one could have helped Jeremiah to be conscious of his purpose except God. If he ever thought of such feat majority would have told him that he was in a fantasy world. God will certainly make you conscious of His will for your life. He will make it so clear to put vision, passion, determination and diligence in your heart. Your consciousness is supposed to serve as a key for optimism, fortitude and doggedness. Consciousness is like self discovery, it empowers and propels you to press into the desire of God for your life. It encourages consistency, gives room for excellence and kindles a fire of fervent prayer that brings such dreams to reality.

Before the advent of Jesus, every sick folk in Israel gathered around the pool of Bethesda in expectation of the angel that troubles the water and opens the door for anyone that goes in first to receive their healing. However, he made His disciples to be conscious of the fact that they have what it takes to heal every form of diseases. This consciousness led to the healing of the man at the beautiful gate, the restoration of the life of Dorcas, the exploit of Philip in Samaria, the transformational ministry and miracles of Paul at Ephesus and the latest dimension in the supernatural feat of servants of God in this contemporary.

God in His mercy never leaves us in darkness. He does everything to bring us to the consciousness of His will. We have people who are still rejecting Jesus as their Lord and personal Saviour yet God has not left them in darkness. He has done everything to make them conscious of the fact that without Christ none can make it to heaven. At Federal Hospital in Kubwa, Abuja Federal Capital Territory in Nigeria, He did something that revealed his will for man's salvation. A girl was born with her hand joins together. The doctors told the parents that they would operate the hands of the girl and give her antistatic. The operation was easy because it seemed that the hands were simply glued together by a single layer of skin and was already one layer apart. When they opened the child's hands, an amazing fact was revealed, because on the inside of the hand the following was written 'JESUS IS COMING BACK!' God used the scene to make people conscious of His will for whoever wants to make it to heaven. What followed? People who had left the church returned and a lot more gave their lives to God.

Being conscious is not accidental, it is borne out of God's operation and purpose for your life. Your consciousness of God's will gives you a greater stand in life and ministry. You will never see the need for persistence without the consciousness of God's will for your life. It paints a picture in your heart. It brings dissatisfaction when you are not thinking and planning towards God's will for your life. It gives a sense of failure despite material possession that is not channeled towards the fulfillment of God's will for your life. Such consciousness carries the power of God that works out His will in your life.

The power of God that brings us to the consciousness of His will for our lives revitalized the life of the following. It raised Gideon from zero to become a hero, Moses form the desert to become a deliverer, Paul from a persecutor to a propagator of the gospel, Sarah from barrenness to a mother of many nations and Thomas from a doubter to a desperate and dutiful disciple who impacted India for Christ. The moment you become conscious of God's will for your life, the giant in you comes alive. It remains the platform where you receive result oriented insight and motivation for your mission on earth.

God may use different sources to bring you to the consciousness of His will. What matters is the fact that it ignites the difference in you.

E – Enclose Fact (God's Will sometimes encloses fact)
God in demonstration of His power to ensure the fulfillment of His will in every ramification did something to make its process a secret to the enemies of progress. He ensured the mind which remains a potential medium of getting information from God for the fulfillment of His will for our lives is not accessible to Satan. Satan is given access into your mind when you are careless in the way you discuss sensitive issues about God's plan for your life with the enemies of progress and fail to resist evil suggestions that come into your mind.

For instance, God never revealed to anyone that the mother of Jesus would be called Mary. Though Joseph was her husband, God did not reveal it to him until later. Elizabeth's knowledge of the fact that Mary was to be the mother of Jesus was to strengthen her faith in God's word and promise for her life. God kept it as a secret from the enemies. Even the wise men did not know that a woman was already pregnant with the Saviour until when He was born.

Why was it concealed? God knew that the world hates change and His birth was to bring an irresistible change to the world. Imagine how challenging it would have been if Herod had knowledge of His conception. It was easy for His parents to move Him from the plot of Herod at His birth. But it would not have been difficult for a pregnant woman to move from one place to another if anyone attempted any evil against her conception. God can do all things. Yes! But it was a wise thing to conceal the conception of Christ in order to avoid attracting unnecessary commotion in Israel at that time.

We must learn from God's wisdom and dealing with man. Do not expose yourself unnecessarily. Allow God to announce His will for your live through His move in your life. And if you need to inform others who are to support you because "a tree does not make a forest", God will inspire you as to who and when to seek help for the fulfillment of His will for your life.

E- Eliminate Enemies (God's will has the power to eliminate enemies)

The key word that God gave to Joshua when he was commissioned was 'fear not'. He knew that he would be faced with great nations and this may likely instill fear. Joshua's reliance on that word gave him victory over 30 kings and he was able to divide the land to the people. No matter how strong those enemies appear to be, your obedience and continuity in God's will empowers you to subdue them. Some finds it difficult to take their stand against the enemy of God's will for their lives. They allow enemies like poverty, fear, prayerlessness, indecision and any other form of foe to stop their journey half way. Remember that nothing is capable of determining your destiny if you are all out to fulfill God's will.

Do not give up on the enemy's plan for your life because of the time you have spent. David's enthronement took 15years; Abraham's child of promise took 25years, Joseph's slavery and imprisonment took 13years before he became the Prime Minister and Jacob's battle between him and Esau took 20years. These people still came to the fulfillment of God's will for their lives despite the time it took. Your focus point should be on the actualization of God's will for your life. God will work things out but if you give up like the children of Israel because of enemies it will be unwise.

We are at an advantaged point over the enemies of God's will, for those of us in Christ. We are sitting in heavenly places in Christ Jesus where all power has been given to us to wield God's will for our lives. The cross, the blood, the word, the name, the nature of Jesus and the key of prayer remains our weapon over every enemy of God's plan and purpose for our lives and family. Be it powers in the sky, on earth and in the sea, we have a greater authority as God's children to push us into God's will for our lives because God delights in silencing the enemies of His will for our lives.

R - Reverse Conclusions (God's will reverses conclusions) *"There are devices in a man's heart, but the counsel of the*

Lord that shall stand."
Every account of evil conclusion against God's will from Genesis to Revelation was paralised by divine reversal. Any evil conclusion stands a chance to fail. That is why in Hebrew 11:35 *"Women received their dead raised to life again..."* Death is the greatest conclusion that any situation on earth can ever experience. If death can be reversed, then no situation can remain impossible. When Satan concluded eternal doom for man by enticing Eve to eat and give her husband, Adam, the forbidden fruit, God reversed it by providing the blood of a lamb and later the blood of Jesus that have opened heaven's gate for man. Pharaoh also concluded in His mind that Israel will never be free from His captivity but God reversed His intention because it was contrary to God's desire. We are all aware of the various concluded issues in the Bible but God reversed every one of them to suit His purpose.

Is God's will for your life facing a threat? Does it seems as if you have come to the end of the road of your life while your purpose is pending? Get your eyes fixed on God. It takes Him nothing to reverse evil conclusions. Wherever such conclusions have been made, He is capable of making such void.

Isaiah 44:24-25 says *"Thus saith the Lord, thy Redeemer, and he that formed thee from the womb, I am the LORD that maketh all things; that stretcheth forth the heavens alone; that spreadeth abroad the earth by myself; That frustrateth the tokens of the liars, and maketh diviners mad; that turneth wise men backward, and maketh their knowledge foolish..."*

If anyone has concluded anything contrary to God's plan for your life, it will be reversed in Jesus' name. Amen.

How does He reverse evil conclusions?
Joel 2:15a "*...sanctify a fast...*" verse 18 says "*Then will the LORD be jealous for his land, and pity his people*" That was exactly what Esther did when Haman with the support of the king has concluded death, shame and destruction contrary to God's plan for the Jews in Shushan. It was fasting and prayer that made God to move the king to taking a step towards Mordecai's promotion instead of destruction. The Bible says that the king could not sleep; he commanded that the record should be brought and be read before him, contrary to His daily routines. And he discovered how Mordecai saved his life yet, he was not rewarded. But that night, after the fasting exercise, God intervened. Whenever believers do not see the need to pray on issues contrary to God's plan for their lives, they seem to be giving access to the enemy to continue to rule over their destiny. God is eager to reverse anything He has not programmed for your life.

R – Raise People Up (God's will raise up people)
The God factor in His will promises supernatural manifestation of God's power. Most people easily come to a conclusion when they are relating with people that seem not to have achieved great feat on earth. They assume that their lives would never experience a turn around. A lot of people in this category have enjoyed God's hand in their lives as He raises them to greater feat in life, Glory to God! It is God's will to raise you up. You can be among the privileged people that God wants to raise up at this time. "*He raiseth up the poor out of the*

dust, and lifteth up the beggar from the dunghill, to set them among princes, and to make them inherit the throne of glory: for the pillars of the earth are the LORD's, and he hath set the world upon them" Never accept tomorrow, downfall, discouragement or frustration. Put them aside, stand on the promises of God and He will raise you up in every area of your life.

Ministerially, maritally, financially and career wise, God is set to raise you up. As you seek God's will with passion, He will raise you up. He will give you idea, revelation, help and a dynamic vision that will take you beyond your imagination.

Do not accept bondage from anyone. Do not allow a man or a woman to keep you from God's will because promotion from man is limiting. Never allow any scorner to talk you out of your calling. Maybe as an instrumentalist, as you continue, God may make of you an instrumentalist that will cast out demons like David. As an evangelist or in your marriage, He will raise you up. If it is God who has called you, He will raise you up. Do not feel shy if things do not seem to be colourful today. He will systematically, turn things around.

Did you just set up a business and you are afraid whether you will be successful or not? If it is indeed God's will, you will encounter possibility. Did you just set up a new ministry or your church sent you to a new location? He will raise your ministry and make His finger known in your life. Someone like Pastor E.A Adeboye became the leader of a denomination of 40 locations and 1500 members in all. Now that God has raised him up, his ministry has gone over 90 nations, richly blessed with excessive wealth. Your obedience to the same God who has done that for him will do it for you. Your calling maybe despised today, fear not, your day of joy is coming because all those who are despising today will celebrate with you at the top.

Chapter Nine

DIVINE ASSISTANCE FOR DOERS OF GOD'S WILL

Divine assistance is awaiting you. Your life will end in praises. God's major duty is to bring the fulfillment of His will to reality. It may be in the life of an individual, a family, city, state, nation or in the world at large. He does not joke with His will, because it represents His authority and purpose on earth. People who deliberately act contrary to His will receive punishment. On the other hand, those who give themselves to God's will receive divine assistance.

Avoid doubting whenever God gives you a directive. Remember, Elijah obeyed God's directive at the time of famine and he was fed by the raven. When the brook got dry he was told to go to the widow of Zarephath and he obeyed. His obedience delivered the woman and her child and allowed God to manifest His power. Many times we hinder God from manifesting His power when we refuse to move in the direction of His will. God is awesome you can only follow Him by faith and serve Him in the spirit. Immediately, you begin to work by sight and allow man's influence every decision you make God will withdraw from you.

God said in 1Kings 17:4b that *"...I have commanded the ravens to feed you there..."* in verse 9b God said *"...I have commanded a widow woman there to sustain thee."* Once God has given a command, it is settled. We must not allow fear or self to hinder us from doing God's will. Believers must put in all it takes to do the will of God. It is only then that all the assistance He has commanded will locate us. If you serve God from this perspective, consecration becomes easy and self denial becomes a lifestyle. God is capable of rendering whatever assistance we need in the fulfillment of His will.

Receiving the Assistance of Angelic Visitation While Doing God's Will.
Give your all to God's will. Anyone whose thoughts, actions, disposition, conversation, passion and supplication is centered on God attracts angelic visitation to themselves.

Do I need the ministry of angels?
It is ignorance to assume that you do not need the ministry of the angels. They operate at God's command to minister to saints. From Genesis, God's people have been enjoying angelic visitation and it will still be relevant till the period of the great tribulation.
What conditions must I meet to enjoy angelic visitation? Strict obedience to God and commitment to His will is all you need to enjoy angelic visitation. Angels do not minister anything good to selfish and disobedient Christians. People in this category who desire angelic visitation are to repent and seek God with all their heart.

The Difference Between The Holy Ghost And The Angels.
- The Holy Ghost is the third person in God while angels run errands.
- The Holy Ghost is involved about our salvation while the angels only rejoice.
- Everyone gets a measure of the spirit of God at conversion while the level of our consecration determines how many angels minister to us.
- The Holy Ghost lives within us while angels stay around us.

- We often bank on the Holy Ghost to fight our battles while angels fight for us at God's command.

I do not expect anyone to pray in the name of angels. The knowledge of angelic ministration to believers is to propel you to a greater level of consecration where angels are assigned to support your purpose on earth.

How To Enjoy The Ministry Of Angels
- Entertain strangers.
- Obey God's directive.
- Contend for the faith.
- Keep yourself holy.
- Wait on the Lord.

- Endure persecution.

(1) Entertain strangers: - *"And there came two angels to Sodom at even; and Lot sat in the gate of Sodom: and Lot seeing them went up to meet them; and he bowed himself with his face toward the ground; And he said, Behold now, my* *lords, turn in, I pray you, into your servant's house and tarry all night and wash your feet and ye shall rise up early, and go your ways. And they said Nay, but we will abide in the street all night. And he pressed upon them greatly, and they turned in unto him and entered his house; and he made a feast, and did bake unleavened bread, and they did eat."* (Gen 19:1-3)

Lot never knew that the step he was taking would result into a great deliverance for him and his family. Lot sat in a position that connected him with angelic visitation. He was quick to discern that they were strangers who needed attention and he exhibited hospitality. May God help us to take steps towards God's mercy and blessings in Jesus' name, amen. Do not be too busy or proud to help people because they were strangers.

David exemplified the necessity of entertaining strangers when he took care of the man he saw on the way while pursuing those who invaded Ziklag and took his possessions and family away. If David had failed to help him he would have missed the information that led to the restoration of his possessions. One who is always less concerned with the needs of others may likely miss the moment of their angelic visitation.

In most places, it is dangerous to help strangers because some have used such an assistance against those who decided to help them. This is why I am appealing that you should walk in the spirit. He knows those whose intention is to hurt us. He speaks and reveals secrets that preserve us from evil. Ensure that you are guided by the spirit where you are rendering assistance to any stranger.

(2) Obey God's directives: *"And the LORD said unto Jacob,*

Return unto the land of thy fathers, and to thy kindred; and I will be with thee" (Genesis 31:3). Your response towards God's directive at every point of your life determines whether the hosts of heaven will attend to you or not. Laban treated Jacob in an unfair manner, yet, he behaved himself and God kept quiet. But when Laban and his family became angry at Jacob God commanded him to return to his father's land (the land of promise) and he obeyed promptly. However, Jacob failed to inform Laban before he departed with his family which would have enabled Laban to bid his daughters and grandchildren fare well. This made Laban to pursue after Jacob. Though, God restrained him from hurting Jacob. He made his grievances known to Jacob. Immediately, they settled and as Jacob *"...went on his way...the angels met him."*

The presence of the angels is an acknowledgement of his obedience towards God's directives. I believe that the angel he wrestled with was among the ones that met him on the way. In the end, it was from the angel he got the blessing. We must ensure prompt obedience to avoid missing our angelic visitation.

(3) Contend for the faith: Elijah was the only prophet in his days who contended for the faith. Contending for the faith cut across every sector of the economy. We must fight against corruption and anything call sin. Be it in education, at the court, fashion designing and so on, we must contend for the faith. People who passionately contend for the faith often enjoys angelic visitation. For Elijah, while *"...he lay and slept under a Juniper tree, behold then an angel touched him."* This was a man that restored true worship to Israel. At this time, he was discouraged and lacked the inner strength required of him to move forward. We thank God that at his weak point, he enjoyed angelic visitation.

(4) Serve God with all your heart: A lady gave a testimony in my church on how she was kidnapped. The men later dropped her at a particular place she was not familiar with. This was because they used charm on her, which made her lose her senses. This made it impossible for her to recognize anyone or anywhere. Fortunately, someone came around and took her to the junction of her house. Those who knew that her family members have been searching for her took her home. To the glory of God, immediately prayer was made for her, she became normal. It pays to serve God with all your heart. You receive an exponential reward in hundred folds and get assistance where you and your family members least expect.

(5) Keep yourself from defilement: *"…in the sixth month (of Elizabeth's conception of John the Baptist) the angel Gabriel was sent from God into a city of Galilee, named Nazareth, To a virgin espouse to a man whose name was Joseph, of the house of David; and the virgin's name was Mary."* (Luke 1:26-27).
Women who received angelic visitation in Bible days kept themselves from every form of defilement. While Elizabeth and her husband lived a holy life despite the challenges of bareness that confronted their family, Mary kept herself as a chaste virgin.

This generation is experiencing a new dimension of response towards sin. Pollution, degeneration and degeneration have been the order of the day in so called assemblies. A lot of bachelors and spinsters are more passionate about marriage than God. This has led to the increase in pre-marital sex. They give up their chastity at the verge of marriage and defile their body which is God's temple. Some still claim that they are born again after defiling their body with immorality. They believe pre- marital sex is a normal thing. The Bible reveals that "...*this is the will of God, even your sanctification that you should abstain from fornication...*" (1Thess 4:3).

People who allow their body to be defiled cannot enjoy angelic visitation. Marriage is a powerful union. God can decide to visit your family. A lot of prayers that people have prayed come to fruition through marriage. God can decide to give you a special child like John the Baptist. You may miss this gift if you defile yourself before marriage. Mary was privilege to become the mother of our saviour because she kept herself from defilement. There are a lot of needs in the world, and from creation God uses marriage, conception, delivery and godliness to raise up those who would serve as solutions to the families, the church, nation or the world at large. This is why you must keep yourself pure as a single. Do not allow the devil to blindfold you of the opportunities that awaits you as a chaste Christian.

(6) Wait on the Lord: God is extremely pleased when His children wait on him. It facilitates the confirmation of angelic visitation in their lives and ministry. Daniel encountered angelic visitation because he waited on the Lord. His prayer set a stage for spiritual warfare between Angel Michael and the prince of Persia and it led to Israel's freedom.

Waiting on the Lord is of utmost importance in the believer's life. You are fortified from within and helped in prayer by the Holy Spirit or angels. Jesus enjoyed such experience at the garden of Gethsemane. He was strengthened by angels to pray through at the hour of prayer.

(7) Endure Persecution: Christianity seems sweet without persecution but God expects us to be mature Christians who earnestly contend for the faith at whatever cost. This is not an easy task. You will be faced with circumstances that are bent to pull you down. Thanks be to God, those who lay their lives down and face situations confronting their faith with the might of Christ always receive angelic visitation. Such was Paul's experience when they met storm on the way for two weeks. Paul did not result into murmuring or complaining to Christ like most Christians. It was such a disposition of patience and trust during persecution that made him to be visited by an angel. That was why he told those in the ship that *"...I exhort you to be of good cheer: for there shall be no loss of any man's life among you, but of the ship. For there stood by me this night the angel of God, whose I am, and whom I serve. Saying, Fear not, Paul; thou must be brought before Caesar: and lo, God hath given thee all them that sail with thee."* (Acts 27:22-24). God does not despise believers who contend for the faith despite persecution. He does everything to assist them.

If you are passing through persecution, expect divine assistance. The only time when believers are left to die in persecution is when it is for God's glory and He has ordained such a persecution like that of Stephen to transport them to heaven.

Chapter Ten

A FULFILLED LIFE

The peak of our existence on earth is measured by fulfillment. The fear of fulfillment has made a lot of people to abandon God's will. Satan plants a picture of failure in their mind if they totally yield themselves to God's will. They assume that anyone who fully commits his or herself to obeying God's will never fulfill his or her destiny. This is why I have decided to concentrate on the possibility of fulfilling your destiny when you give yourself to doing God's will.

A fulfilled life is an evergreen life which is not limited to one's financial or material attainment neither is it a factor of the number of children one is privilege to give birth to. These things are good but it is not an accurate yardstick to measure fulfillment.

Bible based fulfillment can be spelt out as one who:

F - Fights the good fight of faith.

U - Unrelentingly turn many to righteousness,

L - Lays a solid foundation of Christlike influence,

F - Faithfully trains his children in the way of Christ.

I - Intercedes till change occurs,

L- Lavishes his potentials on humanity,

E- Ends at the feet of Christ,
D- Develops others to shine as light.

F- **Fight The Good Fight of Faith**: In our world today, people assume that fulfillment is limited to material things. They make comparison and reckoned with people in relation to their possession.

A close study of Paul's life and ministry reveals the centrality and priority of spiritual and ministerial fulfillment over material fulfillment. He passionately followed through on his ministry to the Gentiles and systematically finished the commission that he received from Christ. Contrary to believers who are contemplating suicide as a result of financial and life's challenges he never complained about lack but courageously declared in 2Tim 4:7 that *"I have fought a good fight, I have finished my course, I have kept the faith."* Therefore, if you are facing financial constraints today while you are obedient to God, do not accept the lie of the devil that you are unfulfilled. God in His faithfulness will soon open the door of your prosperity as you remain diligent and obedient to God's leading.

Faith requires that you abstain from unrighteous gains. Do not give priority to people who take pride in their selfish interest rather than fighting the good fight of faith. God sees anyone who fights the good fight of faith as fulfilled. Your understanding of this fact means that you should continue in God's will when you are faced with rejection, misrepresentation, denial, insults and such likes. Do not follow the pathway of christians who neglect God's will in the pursuance of personal satisfaction. God wants you to be rest assured of a fulfilled life on earth as you give priority to His will. This is as a result of the fact that success originate from Him.

U- **Unrelentingly Turn Many to Righteousness**: - Dan 12:3 *"And they that be wise shall shine as the brightness of the firmament; and they that turn many to righteousness as the stars for ever and ever."*
How consecrated are you to the pursuit of holiness? How passionate are you on total obedience to God? How resolute are you to fight against sin in your life, family and around you?
If you concentrate all your energy on material gain, you may end up in regret when you get to heaven. Material gain is good but should not be substituted with holiness.
Any profession or money venture that contradicts holiness is not for heavenly minded believers. Real fulfillment is tied to your ability to keep holy and assist others to live a holy life while on earth.
This generation is in dare need of those who will lead others in the way of holiness. The Thessalonians became example to people in Macedonia and Achaia because Apostle Paul led them in the way of the Lord.

QUALITIES THAT CAN HELP YOU TURN MANY TO RIGHTEOUSNESS

1. Be determined to stand like Daniel.
2. Be ready to suffer for righteousness sake.
3. Be ready to show love to others.

L- **Lay a Solid Foundation of Christlike Influence**: - A solid foundation that has been laid down to influence humanity in a Christlike manner is the Bible. The Old

Testament was written in Hebrew and Aramaic while the New Testament was written in Greek language. If nothing was done to change the trend, it would have been difficult for the world to know the truth. But someone made a request that stood as the foundation upon which the English Bible was written and the gate for multidimensional usage of the Bible was opened. An everlasting well of refreshing possibility through the scripture was opened. Anyone, anywhere in the world can pick up the Bible at anytime and dig deep into the treasure that heaven has reserved for believers. Whose request made this possible? It was King James's request to have the English version of the Bible that turned the Bible to the bestselling book.

We do not have the details of the glamour of his reign as a king. We do not know how his wife or children look like or the school they attended. We do not know how many houses he built. We do not know how vast he was in business and how massive his estate was. The kind of food he ate, his clothes, friends, cars and possessions make no difference to us. What we can never forget about King James is that his desire for the word of God has led to the advancement in the blessing and knowledge the world has benefitted from the Bible. The literatures that have been written, families that have been built up, conferences that is made possible, sermons preached, souls saved, characters being developed, exploit done due to the revelation gotten from the Bible are immeasurable and innumerable. A lot of accomplishments in other fields of endeavour owe credit to the inspiration gotten from the Bible as Christians. Such attainments would have been difficult if the Bible was not written in English.

We can conclude that the solid foundation of translating the Bible into English which has led to Christ-like influence in the world was a product of King James desire for the Bible.

This is real fulfillment to influence a course that has positively influenced heaven and earth, previous, present and on coming generations positively.

This implies that whenever you are pursuing God's will in laying a good foundation, a solid foundation of Christlike influence, you must remain passionate about it till death. Never allow a feeling of dissatisfaction towards your calling as a result of the opinion of others or the challenges you face at present.

F- Faithfully Trains His Children to Live For Christ: - It will not be a surprising thing if some of the Israelite envied Eli. He held a position in Israel that accorded him a special status. He had the opportunity to enjoy God's blessings and flourished in the prosperity of God's people. Without God's evaluation everyone would have assumed that he will end well. Unfortunately, God judged him because he failed to train his children.

The scripture revealed someone else to us whose fulfillment was not limited to his material possession. He was able to train his children in the way of the Lord. His lifestyle attracted the attention of heaven and God commented it. He did this to set a pace for the generality of Christians in the world so that we do not limit fulfillment to material gain. This all important model is Abraham. In Genesis 18:19 The Bible says: *"...I know him, that he will command his children and his household after him, and they shall keep the way of the LORD, to do justice and judgement; that the LORD may bring upon Abraham that which he hath spoken of him"* God did not judge Eli for personal sins but because of the sins of his children. God expected him to be strict and ensured that his children walked in the fear of the Lord. If he had done that he would have left the world celebrated and not demoted or molested.

We must learn from Abraham and passionately impact our children with the life of Christ. It is one thing to be prosperous in your chosen career and it is another to train your children so they can keep the flag of good morals flying after your departure. A lot of the Children of ministers in contemporary days have been involved in occultism, worldly music, indecent dressing, fraudulent businesses deals, and pre- marital sex. Your children can mar the legacy of excellence you have attained if they lack the fear of God. Therefore we must give priority to training our children in the way of the Lord as we aim at fulfilling our destinies.

Tom Smith at the point of death called his children and advised them to follow his footsteps so they can have peace of mind in life. His daughter, Sara, said: "Daddy, it's unfortunate you are dying without a penny in your bank account. Other fathers that you tag as being corrupt, thieves of public funds left houses and properties for their children; even this house we live in is a rented apartment. Sorry I cannot emulate you, just go and let us chart our own course. " Few months later, Tom Smith died.

Three years later, Sara went for an interview in a multinational company. At the interview, the chairman of the committee asked Sara, "Which Smith are you?" She replied "I am Sara Smith. My father Tom Smith is late." The Chairman cuts in: "O my God! You are Tom Smith's daughter? "He turned to the other members and said, this lady's father was the one that signed my membership form into the institute of administrators and his recommendation earned me where I am today. He did all these free. I did not know his address, he never knew me. He just did it for me. He turned to Sara and said, I have no questions for you, consider yourself as having gotten this job, come tomorrow, your letter will be waiting for you." Sara Smith became the Corporate Affairs Manager of the company with two cars and drivers, a duplex attached to the office, and a salary of One million Euros excluding allowances and other costs.

Two years later, the MD of the company came from America to announce his intension to resign and needed replacement. A personality with high integrity was sought after, again, the company's consultant nominated Sara.

When she was asked the secret of her success in an interview, with tears, she replied, "My Daddy paved these ways for me. It was after he died that I knew he was financially poor but extremely rich in integrity, discipline and honesty." She was asked the reason for her tears since she is not a kid that would still be missing her dad long time after his death. She replied "I insulted my dad at the point of his death for being an honest man of integrity. I hope he will forgive me in his grave now. I did not work for all these, he did". So, finally she was asked, "Will you follow your father's footsteps as he requested?" Her answer was, "I adore the man. He deserves whatever I have after God."

God wants us to leave such a legacy for our children. Do not relegate fulfillment to material or temporal achievement that have made a lot of people to despise God's will.

I- **Intercede till Change occur**: Prayer is power while complaint cripples fulfillment. One with a vibrant prayer life is one who progresses and perfects the will of God on planet earth. The understanding of such individual about fulfillment is different from the majority. They desire the fulfillment of God's will in the lives of others as well as in their own lives. They have learnt how to wield the weapon of intercessory prayers to ensure the fulfillment of God's will in the world. This is the tool that made Daniel's fulfillment legendary. Other people like Nehemiah, Whitefield, John Knox, Apostle Babalola, Esther, etc. unlocked the treasures of heaven, stormed humanity with the legacy of dynamic possibility through the explosive power of intercessory prayers.

The word change has always been a product of intercessory prayers. The Christian world has not known any sustained change outside the four walls of intercession.
When you get to this level, your prayer affects eternity, humanity and brings about the multiplicity of the influence of the divine force of the Trinity in our society. This indeed is a fulfilled life. You might say it is just a part

of fulfillment. Remember that a part makes up a whole.

It is a known fact that one who prays through to breakthrough must surely come like David to a stable round table of all round rest and fulfillment.

Words works wonders at the hour of prayer
The productive force of your words and creative force of God's word coupled with the ultimate trust in God's will actualizes the unimaginable when utilized prayerfully. It was this force that brought the emergence of reformation in Scotland by John Knox. Like a ladder, he climbed the high tower of prayer for thirteen years saying "Give me Scotland or I die" No fulfillment can outshine the reformation he brought to Scotland.
It is a pity that this generation of Christians counts prosperity as the peak of fulfillment and has failed to pursue the highly treasured divine fulfillment that is capable of affecting eternity.

The Indispensability of Intercessory Prayer

"... I sought for a man among them, that should make up the edge, and stand in the gap before me for the land, that I should not destroy it: But I found none. Therefore, I have poured out mine indignation upon them..." (Ezekiel 22:30-31)
Intercessory prayer is the source of the light of exponential revival that is shining among Christian fold in Africa. We have those who mistakenly assume that Africans are naturally religious that is why they gather in hundreds of thousands to fellowship before the Lord. No, any true minister will testify of intense prayer and

fasting that went ahead before the light of fire of revival shone and attracted multitude towards their ministry.

The sight of the supernatural move of God in His house agrees to the fact that interceding till change comes is one of the greatest fulfillments an individual can attain on earth. What achievement can be compared to the fulfillment of deliverance from sin, kidney failure, demonic oppression, insanity, bareness, HIV, elephantiasis, blindness, poverty, paralysis and problems like divorce receiving solutions? You know that personal accomplishment in real estate, automobile, communication, banking, education and others does not outweigh the feat intercessory prayer of God's servants has earned.

In Ezekiel 22: 30-31, God did not lament because there was no mansion in the land. Marriages were not taking place or women were not giving birth. He lamented because intercessory prayer that shielded the land from God's wrath was missing. E.A Adeboye (the General overseer of Redeemed Christian Church of God) gave his testimony on how to his church grew. He said at the beginning of his ministry, he would invite great ministers to his church so can gather great crowd. But immediately those ministers go, the crowd also go away. Later, he decided to change his method. He discovered in the book of Act that the basis of church growth is miracles. He gathered his team and went into a lengthy period of prayer programme. This has eventually led to his Church being the biggest and richest in the world. And this feat has been maintained through intercessory prayers.

All encompassing change through intercession

Some things will not happen except there is constant intercession. Nehemiah never knew the level of change that could occur in Jerusalem when he commenced his prayer. We must follow through on the burden of prayer born out of the passion we have in our hearts for the manifestation of God's will. *"The words of Nehemiah the son of Hakaliah. And it came to pass in the month Chisleu, in the twentieth year, as I was in Shushan the palace. That Hanani, one of my brethren, came, he and certain men of Judah, and I asked them concerning the Jews that had escaped, which were left of the captivity, and concerning Jerusalem. And they said unto me, The remnant which are left of the captivity there in the province are in great affliction and reproach: the wall of Jerusalem also is broken down, and the gates thereof are burned with fire. And it came to pass, when I heard these words, that I sat down and wept, and mourn certain days, and fasted, and prayed before the God of heaven."*(Nehemiah 1:1-4). The resultant effect of the prayer of Nehemiah which was due to the burden he had for Israel was an unimaginable change. The burden he had which led to this prayer can be called sorrow of the heart. Most ministers advise their members to despise any form of sorrow of heart that arises when they have certain problems in their lives. To a little extent, that may be correct but sorrow of heart has helped a great number of people to push in prayer into God's will till lasting change occurred. Amongst such individuals are Hannah, Joshua, Jacob and Jesus. The degree of sorrow in your heart increases the intensity, fervency and continuity in prayer.

The Reality of Unlimited Change through your burden (passion) for God's will

- Hannah had Samuel.
- Nehemiah found favour before Artaxarxes.
- Esther rescued the Jews from destruction.
- Jesus' fulfilled His purpose for humanity.
- Nehemiah experienced unlimited change through intercession

The burden of prayer for the supernatural in you is a seed of destiny that would affect many generations. More so, the urgency applied in issue that requires emergency determines your worth in God's army. Never be slack in handling challenges because the life of a conqueror is a product of challenges. A force of victory and change follow you anytime you intercede or pray.

You must be aware that the prayer that will give rise to lasting change will demand more from you. It demanded focus from Hannah, leaping from Jacob, sweat like blood from Jesus and consistency from Nehemiah. You can get more than what you expect. This was the experience of Nehemiah, He aimed at building the walls of Jerusalem but went further than that to become the governor of God's people. In conclusion:

1. He built the walls,
2. He relieved their burden of oppression.
3. He set faithful men over Jerusalem.
4. He motivated others to contribute sacrificially.
5. He restored the law and true worship to Israel.
6. He established unity in Jerusalem.
7. He helped others like Ezra to fulfill their teaching ministry.
8. He separated the mixed multitude from Israel.
9. He stopped unequal yoke in marriage in Jerusalem.

The change that comes through constant intercession cannot be over emphasized. This is the picture of true fulfillment.

L- Lavishes His potential on his generation

You need not to be afraid whenever your stand for God's will attracts opposition, rejection, demotion and temporary starvation. You can accomplish 100 fold as you contend for the will of God. You may sometimes lose friends or your job. Yet, that does not cancel your fulfillment in life. The component that takes us to the platform of fulfillment amidst challenges is our potential. While some people dread God's will because they are not certain of the possibility embedded in it, others attain unimaginable height of fulfillment through the usage of their potentials. God ensures the empowerment of whosoever seeks His will. He helps them to discover and maximize their potential in a grand style. Martin Luther's potential gave birth to the American dream. Myles Munroe's potential left amazing write ups for humanity.

The height potentials take dreams is greater than the height lift can take men. Potential is a cross continental product without which every other thing will paralyze. It gives beauty to man's existence on the planet earth. Every nation, organization, denomination and so on gives credence to potential. The value of a potential that is developed is worth more than a skyscraper in a city. This is because potential can have impacts on eternity and pave the way for coming generations to walk on the red carpet of wonders. Thomas Edison's potential has provided a good ground for the advancement of the twenty-first century. It has made the gospel to penetrate into different countries of the world. There would be a limitation to our level of usefulness in the kingdom without the functionality of potentials. Such may be innate or imparted.

Examples of potential in you.
1. The word of knowledge (imparted)
2. The word of wisdom (imparted)
3. Discerning of spirit (imparted)
4. Inspiring writing skills.
5. Information Technology.
6. Oration.
7. Musical skill.
8. Hospitality.
9. Science.
10. Creative art.

These and many more are examples of potentials that can enable you
to influence the world.

A fulfilled life never dies with their potential unutilized to maximum level. Myles Munroe had a strong believe on dying empty. If you fail to fully utilize your potential before death, you have deprived humanity of a seed of change.
Elijah's potential was lavished on Elisha, Christ's on the disciples and humanity, Paul's potential on Asia Minor.

Who will you lavish your potential on?
Some people's estate would be wasted by prodigal sons who inherited them. But a potential that is transferred will reflect God's glory and reproduce 100 fold blessings. This is the bone and source of enduring success. Great ministers testify to this. Pastor Oyedepo testified to the influence of Pastor Kenneth Hagin's and Pastor Adeboye's potential on his ministry. There are people whose fulfillment depends solely on the effective use of your potential. It is a treasure that is worth more than silver and gold.

The Forces that transfer Potential
(a) Your words.
(b) Your writings.
(c) Your way of life.
(d) Your warfare.

(a) Your Words transfer potential
"THE HAND of the LORD was upon me, and carried me out in the Spirit of the LORD, and set me down in the midst of the valley which was full of bones. And caused me to pass by them round about: and, behold, there were very many in the open valleys; and, lo, they were very dry. And he said unto me, Son of man, can these bones live? And I answered, O Lord God, thou knowest. Again he said unto me, Prophesy upon these bones, and say unto them, O ye dry bones, hear the word of the LORD". (Eze 37:1-4)
Man was created in God's image. This confers man's word with the potential and creative power in God's word. Your word is one of the greatest potentials needed for a systematic and remarkable touch on lives and destinies. Every global, national and societal challenges

encountered in our daily lives will experience change if only we utilize our words to command normalcy.

Ezekiel was brought to the valley of dry bone which could be liken to the hopeless state of the economy of most countries, increasing number of divorce in the world, the depth of occultism in our campus, the level of corruption in our country and the influence of sin in our society. Like many of us Ezekiel did not believe that anything could happen to the dry bones until God said, prophesy. That means that the potential that is needed for the miraculous is in your words. Thank God for Ezekiel, he made use of his potential. He said, *"So I prophesied as he commanded me, and the breath came into them, and they lived and stood upon their feet an exceeding great army"*. (Eze 37:10) An exceeding great army of peaceful people can rise from a society filled with violence. An exceeding great army of prosperity replaces poverty; an exceeding great army of people known for purity can emerge from a filthy community and productivity from an unproductive subordinate. Your word has the potential to change a cloudy weather of discouragement to a clear weather of courage and creativity. Nehemiah used it and the wall of Jerusalem was rebuilt. Napoleon Hill used it and prisoners were rehabilitated. Nigerian nationalist used it and it gave rise to independence in Nigeria. Our Lord Jesus used it and His disciples became apostles who turned the world upside down for good.

The potential in man's word is the reason for all the seminars, crusades, church services, television and radio programmes that are organised to release a steady flow of a dynamic influence on others and in order to develop a positive attitude that unleashes the light of God's will in the world. Your word is a seed of destiny, judiciously make use of it.

(b) **Your writings transfer potential:** -Myles Munroe shared his experience on how he was propelled to become a prolific writer who wrote inspiring materials that triggered vision, passion and knowledge. He said while he was handling a motivational show on television, he was advised to put it in writing. This will sustain the relevance of his ideas and ingenuity after his death. He did exactly that, and became as it is today one of the authors whose books are among the best-selling books. Unfortunately, he died in a plane crash with his wife and one of their children but his books still impact knowledge.

The world can never forget great authors like Napoleon Hill, Anthony Robbins, John C. Maxwell, Dr David Oyedepo and many others who rode on the tip of their fingers into people's lives and imparted destinies of people they had never seen.

The faintest ink is sharper than the sharpest brain. The potential in writing has produced uncountable professors, surgeons, doctors, lecturers, lawyers, teachers to mention a few.

Furthermore, God established the knowledge of His kingdom and His programme for humanity through writing. This started from the mount where Moses wrote the Ten Commandments. The potential in writing has advanced and made the invention of the internet to be possible. This has afforded men to gain access to the best information that serves as a solution on every endeavour, challenge and ambition.

Have you been thrilled by the performance of musicians who sing classic? Most of those songs were written in the 16th, 17th, 18th, or 19th century. And this could not have been made possible without writing. As I round up this topic, I would like to share the experience of a man of God with you. He is a pastor in one of the biggest churches in the world. He said that the General Overseer of his ministry gave him a topic to preach at their minister's conference where over 15000 leaders from everywhere in the world meet for preparation for maximum impart in ministry. Unfortunately, he did not have any idea about the topic. So he went to see the principal of the Bible school of that ministry in Lagos who referred him a particular book. To his amazement, the topic he had struggled with without solution was made easy through the information he got from the chapter one of that book. No one can exhaust the potential embedded in writing.

(c) **Your way of life transfers potential**: Action speaks louder than words. Your action is the potential that influences others even when you are in silence. Your knowledge accomplishes more when it corresponds with your action. You influence people who are far away through your words (messages or seminars), and writing and through your way of life (character). Your reaction to situations around sends a message to them, and through observation, they open up to the impartation of your potential on their lives. They take your sitting position, the tone of your voice while talking and your attitude in general as a standard for their lives. This is what enabled Gideon to lead 300 men to battle and defeat the multitude of Midianites and Amalekites. He simply said *"...Look on me, and do likewise: and, behold, when I come to the outside of the camp, it shall be that, as I do, so shall ye do."* (Judges 6:17)

The potential of a man of valour that was upon him was transferred as they observed his actions. Paul also, testified that his courage during persecution emboldened others to preach the gospel.

You must have experienced a great and a sustained change before you can control people through your actions. The decision of our Lord Jesus to accept crucifixion for man's salvation affected the disposition of the disciples positively. They all, except John, the beloved laid lay down their lives for the gospel.

What are your actions like?
Are they igniting passion in others or influencing them negatively? One whose actions influence people positively is fulfilled.

Where is your action leading others?
Is it leading them towards heaven, greatness or to failure and to the bottomless pit? Your actions are the history of your life that is written in the minds of people and it will last for all eternity.

(c) **Your warfare transfers potential**

Warfare here means going the extra mile in prayer to rescue difficult situations. This is what Jesus meant when he said *"Simon, Simon, behold, Satan hath desired to have you, that he may sift you as a wheat: But I have prayed for thee that thy faith fail not: and when thou art converted strengthened thy brethren."* (Luke 21:31-32). The potential of the prayer of Jesus brought about the possibility of his restoration after his fall. The potential of your warfare can save a whole generation. Warfare is the weapon used by believers to expand God's kingdom and subdue the domination of darkness over the generality of humanity. The potential in the prayer of Daniel restored Israel after seventy years of bondage in Egypt, Peter from the destructive plan on Herod, John knox transformed Scotland to Christ.

The instrumentality of the potential in warfare has created an atmosphere leading to resurrection of lost destinies, release of Satan's captives, conversion of filthy sinners and built lasting ministries. No church or believer can be fulfilled or aid the fulfillment in others without proper utilization of the potential in warfare. *"For we wrestle not against flesh and blood but against principalities, against the rulers of darkness of this world, against spiritual wickedness in high places"* (Eph 6:12) The act of wrestling is nom-negotiable because *"...though we walk in the flesh, we do not war after the flesh: (For the weapon of our warfare are not carnal, but mighty through God to the pulling down of strong holds:) Casting down imaginations, and every high thing that exalteth itself against the knowledge of God, and bringing into captivity every thought to the obedience of Christ"* (2 Cor 10:3-5). You cannot make use of the weapon of warfare without being involved in the act of warfare.

I learnt of a seventy years old man who was highly intelligent but very poor. Fortunately, as a Christian, he was made a secretary in his church. At a time, it was observed that he never pen down anything during the course of the meeting, and still gives the minute of meeting in details word for word. This called the attention of the ministers, who were forced to ask the reason for his poverty with such a level of intelligence that he possesses. They proceeded to praying for him. It was then that it was discovered that when he was young, his mother took him to an Ifa priest to foretell his destiny. The Ifa told her that the boy would live among the whites. Due to her ignorance, she felt the boy would abandon her. Therefore, she told the man to do something that will hinder the manifestation of the boy's destiny. The man did his enchantment, tied it and threw it into the sea. This made this man to be stagnant for 70 years. But, thanks be to God, after the prayer of the men of God: the programme of darkness for his destiny was reversed. Surprisingly, he traveled at seventy.

Warfare remains a major way of transferring the potential for greatness and fulfillment into people's lives, developing it accomplishes incredible feats.

Coming back to where we started from, a fulfilled life is one that;

L-Looks out for God's will in the church It is a pity that many people today handle the church like personal business venture. This is why politics and tradition of the elders rather than God's will is the order of the day in many churches.

God expects every minister to seek God's will in all things.

We would consider three of such. They are;
(1) Leadership
(2) Doctrine
(3) Finance

Fulfilling God's will in appointing leaders "...*THE LORD said unto Samuel, How wilt thou mourn for Saul, seeing I have rejected him from reigning over Israel? Fill thine horn with oil, and go, I will send thee to Jesse the Bethlehemite: for I have provided me a king among his sons...And it came to pass, when they were come, that he looked on Eliab, and said, surely the LORD'S anointed is before him. But the LORD said unto Samuel, look not on his countenance, or on the height of his stature; because I have refused him: for the LORD seeth not as man seeth: for man looketh on the outward appearance, but the LORD looketh on the heart.*" (1 Samuel 16:1, 6-7).

God is greatly delighted whenever His servants consult Him before choosing leaders in His vineyard. This is of utmost importance because the selection of leaders in Bible days was based on God's call for such individual.
The strategic call for leadership should not be handled with levity but should be pioneered by the Holy Spirit. This is what Christ pictured that made him to pray all night before selecting His choice of leaders. Similarly, the leaders at Antioch waited on the Lord before choosing Barnabas and Saul for the mission work. This is why their ministry was accompanied with signs and wonders.

All churches must go back to this method of choosing leaders, if she desires the miraculous as in days gone by.

Any church that puts God aside in the selection of leaders will miss out from God's programme for the church. He is ever ready to assist the church in the selection of leaders that will take such churches to the realm of glory that God has ordained for the next generation. Churches that give priority to financial status, family background, facial appearance rather than auction to function while searching for leaders cannot claim to be faithful to God's will. God's choice may be rich or otherwise, but it will lead to the advancement of God's purpose for the church. The church will experience advancement in holiness, exploit, perfection and domination of the land.

Fulfilling God's will in doctrine: - Doctrine determines the direction and influence that the church has over its members. It demands proper knowledge and conviction of the truth in the scripture.

Leaders who took time to search the scriptures and lay a solid foundation of scriptural conviction and holiness; have been able to depopulate the kingdom of darkness and increase heaven bound saints. Your doctrine determines the strength of your church. It serves as a standard for every member of the church to follow. It also helps to determine the ministerial and spiritual progress of the church. A populated church without sound doctrine is like a church that is dead spiritually. Anointing multiplies membership while doctrine multiplies righteousness and discipline in the church.

A fulfilled minister in the light of the aforementioned is one who builds the body of Christ on the whole truth.

Ministers who are striving for the Christ-like fulfillment

and not momentary compliments give themselves to the study of scripture and preaching of the truth. The greatest mistake a minister would ever make is to replace Christ-like fulfillment which is centered on the truth of the gospel with earthly gain. That is why Christ told the angel in the church of Pergamos that "...*I have a few things against thee, because thou hast there them that hold the doctrine of Balaam, who taught Balac to cast a stumbling block before the children of Israel, to eat things sacrificed unto idols, and to commit fornication so hast thou also them that hold the doctrine of the Nicolaitans, which thing I hate.*" (Rev2:14)

What kind of doctrine are you spreading?
Is it a doctrine that propels inward and outward purity or the doctrine of Balaam that allow women to put on nude dresses, tight trousers and mini skirt to Church? These things promote lust in the church. That is why many youths cannot stand for the Lord and many ministers are committing immorality either physically or in the heart.
I once met a young man who told me that his pastor always faces up whenever he is preaching. He was forced to ask why? The man told him that was the only way he could keep himself from lusting.
What is the place of the word of God in the mouth of a minister? Is it not to sanitise the church? Unfortunately, many people make the people happy and not holy. They do not understand that ministry is different from mere activity. Activity is limited to the physical while ministry influences our spiritual life and prepares us for heaven. A fulfilled ministry leaves a lasting impact on the spiritual realm of its members and in the world.

Fulfilling God's will in Finance: *"LET A man so account of us, as of the ministers of Christ, and stewards of the mysteries of God. Moreover it is required in stewards that a man be found faithful."*

A fulfilled steward is that person who ensures that he is not defiled with church funds. Those who have access to either count, deposit or are even assigned to take some money to do something should ensure they are faithful.

The book of Deuteronomy 17 from verse 14-17 says: *"when thou art come unto the land which the Lord thy God giveth thee, and shalt possess it, and shalt dwell therein, and shall say, I will set a king over me, like as all the nations that are about me: Thou shalt in any wise set him king over thee, whom the LORD thy God shall choose: one from among thy brethren shalt thou set king over thee ... he shall not multiply wives to himself, that his heart turn not away: neither shall he greatly multiply to himself silver and gold"* This gives the picture of God's will as regards church leaders, and church funds. No minister is permitted to use church funds for extravagant living. Tithes and offerings are different from gifts given to you as a leader. We must ensure that luxurious goods whose purchase and maintenance will drain the finances of the church should be avoided. These are not basic needs so, moderation is possible.

The bigger the finance of your church, the bigger your vision to possess the land should be. It affords us to simultaneously push and turn the world upside down for Christ.

E- Ends at the feet of Christ

Fulfillment without making it to heaven is incomplete. Do not seek fulfillment that is not all encompassing.

This should serve as an encouragement whenever you are facing temptations that want to kill your faith. When you meet with people who want to kill your passion for God's will as a result of their achievements, individuals who assume that fulfillment is limited to their opinions and make you feel inferior because you have not achieved what the world applauds, let it ring in your heart that real fulfillment is getting to heaven.
Increase your drive to end at the feet of Jesus. A lot of people will do everything to divert your attention. Remember that nothing is as important as making heaven. Believe me, no fulfillment can be equated to such.

We must not allow the joy of God's blessings, responsibility and difficulties of discipling others to hinder us from focusing our eyes on heaven. This is because in the end, all the plaudits, popularity, and wow presentations or preaching will make no meaning if you do not make it to the feet of Jesus.

A fulfilled believer is not one who depends on his earthly accomplishments but, one who ensures that his or her relationship with Christ is intact. This was apostle Paul's experience when he said *"I have fought a good fight, I have finished my course, I have kept the faith: Henceforth there is laid up for me a crown of righteousness, which the Lord, the righteous judge, shall give me at that day: and not to me only, but unto all them that love his appearing."* (2 Tim 4:7-8) God wants this to be our testimony.

Do not give up your faith because you want to get married to a particular man or woman. You may end up getting yourself hooked up with such an individual that makes you feel fulfill but if you do not finish your Christian race in heaven that marriage is actually a failure no matter the things you seem to be enjoying.

Do not allow people who would do anything to get promotion, money, favour, contracts, position and every good thing that this world can afford. Those people who do such do not have a true picture of fulfillment. Though, they seem to be blindfolded and boastful of their assumed success that has taken them away from the Lord. Most Christians cannot stand the sight of such people. They somehow adore them deep in their hearts, they fail to see the destruction awaiting such people. A lot of Christians in this category fight with the temptation to backslide because they constantly desire the wealth and the pleasures of sinners. Gehazi, Judas and Demas are good examples of such people.

D- **Develop others to shine as light:** Development demands the involvement of visionaries who see fulfillment as incomplete until they reproduce themselves in others. This is the greatest of all accomplishments in every continent. The estate one leaves for children, the certificate gotten, the fame that made you a celebrity, will be of no relevance to eternity and humanity if you are not able to impact others with the qualities that made you achieve the extraordinary. This is the key that unlocks the potential of the next generation.

Jesus did not ascend until He developed the disciple to continue the commission He started. Paul inculcated the virtue of an evangelist in Timothy and many others before he said *"...I am now ready to be offered, and the time of my departure is at hand."* (2 Tim 4:6) Elijah was not taken to heaven in the Chariot until he anointed Hazael as king over Syria, Jehu as king over Israel and Elisha a prophet in the room of Elijah. More so, Moses reproduced the conquering spirit in him in Joshua before his death.

The level of your influence or impact either in the body of Christ or in the secular world is dependent on the numbers of people whose lives received a transforming touch through you. Developing others enables you to reach a large number of people in a short time. Pastor W. F kumuyi's ministry has reached 60 nations as at 2014 and that of Pastor E. A Adeboye 90 nations in 2017. They cannot attain such a height without developing others.
The price you pay for developing others is your selfless contribution to the expansion of God's kingdom and the elevation of the quality of life of the people. This guarantees the bright future that we desire in every country.

This is the picture of a fulfilled life that God wants us to have. You do not need to be a pastor before developing others. All you need is dedication and commitment in the development of others in your area of expertise. You must ensure that you serve as an example in purity, justice and tranquility. Your impact in drama, education, science, law, government, mass media and every other body; makes eternity to increase in number and the world better.

Chapter Eleven

IDENTIFYING THE ENEMIES OF GOD'S WILL

Ministry is different from activity. Ministry changes destiny but activity entertains emotion. God's will is equated with ministry because it always fulfills a glorious purpose in the life of many.

The will of God for Joseph to be taken to Egypt rescued his generation from famine. God's will for the coronation of David gave Israel rest from battles. God's will to make Paul an Apostle has brought the light of salvation and God's glory to gentile nations. And God's will that made Jesus our saviour brought beauty to man's pursuit of worshipping God.

The basis of my explanation is to establish the fact that the advantages attached to God's will attract enemies who are positioned by Satan to fight the fulfillment of God's will in the world.

I will like to summarise enemies of God's will into three;

- *Physical enemies*
- *Spiritual enemies*
- *Psychological enemies*

Physical Enemies: Physical enemies constitute the company of those you interact with in your daily activities. And it includes constituted authorities that Satan sometimes uses to resist God's will within their sphere of influence.

The decision of Peter and John to press into God's will in prayer and healing was faced with reaction from the Sadducees and the priests who commanded them to be imprisoned.

God wants you to have a strong resolve for His will. You must be resolute because you will be faced with circumstances that intend to weaken your drive to fulfill God's will. Examples of such enemies can be found in the following:

- Hatred as in the case of the brothers. (Gen 37:8)
- Wrong counsel as in the case of Job's wife. (Job 2:9)
- Temptation of immorality as in the case of Potiphar's wife. (Gen 39:12)
- Oppression as in the case of King Zedekiah to Jeremiah. (Jeremiah 32: 3)
- Reproach as in the case of Jesus Christ on the cross. (Luke 23: 35-39)
- Critical attitude and obstruction to your progress like Saballat and Tobiah (Nehemiah 4:1)
- Disappointment as in the case of Jacob and Laban when he served for seven years for Racheal.

Spiritual Enemies: The spiritual influences the physical. Spiritual enemies stage events that are aimed at countering the will of God in all ramifications. These are *"...principalities, powers, rulers of darkness of this world,* *spiritual wickedness in high places...*" (Ephesians 6:12). These enemies operate everywhere. But glory be to God that Christ has conquered darkness and has positioned us to reign and rule in His stead. We have been empowered from on high to silence these enemies.

You must be watchful, ignorance is dangerous and unbelief gives Satan legal ground. You must be on the offensive to triumph.

Psychological Enemies: Psychology deals with the mind and one's emotions. The major players of such enemies are fear, unbelief, discouragement, procrastination, laziness and lack of confidence.

The picture that is painted in your mind is capable of destroying or activating your destiny. These enemies painted a picture of grasshopper in the mind of the Israelites which made them to perish in the wilderness. The picture that was painted in Esau's mind made him to sell his birthright. Saul had the picture of defeat painted in his mind due to lack of confidence in God. This made him to make a sacrifice which was not supposed to offer.

The major key of victory over psychological enemies is being grounded in God's word and prayer. It increases God's grace in your life and helps you to mount up on eagle's wings at the face of any challenge that is aimed at posing unbelief, fear, doubts and lack of confidence before you.

The Weapons Against the Enemies of God's will

- The cross.
- Christ's crucifixion.
- The creative word.
- Your conviction.

(1) The Cross: The cross is the gateway of the victory

of Christians all over the world. It ushered humanity into a realm of permanent victory. This was confirmed in Christ utterance on the cross, when He said "...it is finished..." (John 19: 30b). This utterance has the same power with that of Genesis 1:3 when "...God said, Let there be light: and there was light." *The same way the voice produced a light of a new dawn, so also, the voice of the Son accomplished wonders in Matthew 27: 50-51b. It states that "Jesus, when he had cried again with a loud voice, the veil of the temple was rent in twain from the top to the bottom; and the earth did quake, and the rocks rent."* Christ's triumphant utterance coupled with the might of His crucifixion can rent any veil of long time barrier, shake the powers of this world and rent difficulties that seem to be confronting the will of God for your life like the rock that hinders the passage of anything that want to go through it.

(2) Christ's Resurrection: Resurrection unleashed a possibility that is beyond man's imagination. It broke the order that places the dead body permanently in the grave. It projected man to a higher pedestal in our relationship with God. Man was promoted to a realm of greater possibilities in purity and power.

Resurrection reflected the totality of God's power. It beats the enemy hands down. Eph 1:19-20 says: *"What is the exceeding greatness of his power to us-ward who believes according to the working of his mighty power. Which he wrought in Christ when he raised him from the dead, and set him at his own right hand...Far above principalities, and power..."* The miracle of Christ's resurrection brings every enemy under my feet. It has raised us to a new realm where we wield the fullness of God's power.

What happened at resurrections remains an awesome

spiritual weapon for God's will. Matthew 28:2 *"...there was a great earthquake*: (Every ground the enemy is standing on to operate in your life rends through resurrection power) *for the angel of the Lord descended from heaven and rolled back the stone from the door...*(You experience angelic intervention that overthrows every obstacles to God's will for your life) *for the fear of him* (God will put your fear in your enemies) *the keepers did shake,* (every power monitoring you will be shaken) *and became as dead men."*(The enemies of your fulfillment and their weapon will be paralysed). You are positioned at an advantage point in winning spiritual battles.

(3) The Creative Word: *"IN THE beginning was the Word, and the Word was with God, and the Word was God...All things were made by him, and without him was not anything made that was made."*(John 1:1, 3)

God wants us to utilize the weapon of the creative power in the word. Christians must be grounded in the knowledge of God's word as agents of darkness give priority to incantation. Jesus himself triumphed over Satan through the instrumentality of the word. The reason is that *"...the word of God is quick, and powerful, and sharper than any two edged sword..."* (Heb 4:12). A believer who is loaded with the scriptures in addition to holy living will have a piercing effect on the enemy as he utilizes God's word in battle. While a believer without an in depth knowledge of the word of God is like a believer without a sword. Its creative power turns things around. Learn to use it against difficult situations.

(4) Your Conviction:

Conviction is the force that gives birth to:

- Resurrection in Christ.
- Triumph over Hitler in Winston Churchill.

- Invention of air flying machine in the Wright Brothers.
- Transformation of South Africa in Nelson Mandela.
- Unquenchable passion for human rights in Martin Luther.

Truly the list is endless. Nothing worthwhile can be achieved without the aid of a fire packed conviction.

This implies that the challenges confronting the fulfillment of God's will for your life can be subdued if you keep your conviction alive. A conviction that is alive is an all out conviction that turns difficult circumstances to experiences that produce wisdom to restrategise.

How to Keep Your Conviction Alive

1. Study the scriptures: These are promises that reassure your hope on God's will.

2. Consecrate your future: Great revelation and insight come through consecration.

3. Follow divine guidance: God will lead you to people and places that will facilitate the
fulfillment of His will for your life.

4. Press on in prayer: This is the stage in the production process of our purpose where
personal feeling is separated from divine leading and unrealistic pursuit give way for a
new dawn of clearer revelation of God's will.

The aforegoing set your conviction on fire and renew your strength to patiently work out God's will for your life.

Dakarabor .O. David studied Economics/ Computer in Michael Otedola College of Education. He is a prolific and gifted writer. He is presently a student of NOUN (National Open University of Nigeria) and also a member of Data Processing Management of Nigeria.

He is a dynamic writer whose writing facilitates divine awakening in readers. He is set to use his systematic and expository writing skills to establish a platform that would aid the perfection of God's purpose in this and coming generations.

About The Book

God's will is central to God's dealing with man. He gives priority to His will in every ramification. His plans are inexhaustible. It covers every area and seconds of our lives.

The fact that God has reserved unlimited treasures for man requires that we have in-depth knowledge of His will which will enable us gain access into His plan for our lives and avoid diversions or distractions and delay.

The author has been able to give an elaborate explanation that is corroborated with Biblical and experiences of contemporary men and women.

He has thoroughly expatiated on;
Definition of God's will.
Insight into God's will,
Wonders of God's will,
How to find and know God's will,
Sacrifice for God's will,
The key into God's will,
The test of God's will,
The power of God's will,
Divine assistance of doers of God's will,
The enemies of God's will, and
Weapon against the enemies of God's will.